Introduction

If you love the soft touchable yarns that are available, but would like to knit something other than a scarf with them, this book is for you!

These sweaters are definitely designed for speed without losing any points in the style department. Whether you are looking for a jacket that can go anywhere or a scene-stealing topper that will make an outfit shine, you'll find it in this collection.

We have included what yarn we used for our photographed styles. But if you are in love with a similar yarn that's the same weight, we encourage you to make a swatch with it, check your gauge, and substitute the yarn you love. Information is included on page 35 on checking gauge.

Si a usted le gustan los estambres suaves al tacto que ahora están disponibles, pero quisiera tejer con ellos algo más que una simple bufanda, ¡este libro es para usted!

Estos suéteres han sido diseñados en nuestro departamento de diseño para que sin duda usted pueda avanzar rápidamente y sin perder puntos. Ya sea que usted esté buscando un saco que pueda llevar a todos lados o un top que robe cámaras para iluminar su vestuario, usted lo encontrará en esta colección.

Hemos incluido el tipo de estambre que utilizamos en nuestros estilos fotografiados, pero si usted está enamorada de otro estambre similar del mismo peso, le recomendamos hacer una muestra con él, verificar su punto, y sustituir con el estambre que usted desee. Se incluye información en la página 35 sobre como verificar su muestra de punto.

Contents

Contenido

On the Town Jacket
Saco En el Pueblo 2

Go-Everywhere Jacket
Saco para Ir a Todas Partes 6

Be-Ribboned Shrug
Chaqueta Encintada 10

Comfy Little Topper
Pequeño Top Cómodo 14

Fur-Collar Cardi
Chaqueta de Punto con Cuello de Piel 18

Light as Air Cropped Jacket
Saco Corto Ligero como el Viento 22

Quick & Easy Tee
Blusa Fácil y Rápida 26

Must-Have Tunic
Túnica Tengo Que 29

Easy-to-Wear V-Neck
Cuello en V Fácil de Usar 32

On the Town Jacket

Saco En el Pueblo

Skill Level

EASY

Sizes

Woman's small (medium, large, extra-large, 2X-large) Instructions are given for smallest size, with larger sizes in parentheses. When only 1 number is given, it applies to all sizes.

Finished Measurements

Chest: 41 (44, 48, 54, 60) inches

Materials

- Patons Carmen bulky weight yarn (1.75 oz/64 yds/50g per skein): 9 (10, 11, 12, 13) skeins camel #07010
- Size 10½ (6.5mm) knitting needles
- Size 11 (8mm) knitting needles or size needed to obtain gauge
- 2 plastic markers
- Purchased flower pin (optional)
- Large snap set

5 BULKY

Gauge

12 sts and 14 rows = 4 inches/10 cm in St st
To save time, take time to check gauge

Nivel de dificultad

FÁCIL

Tallas

Dama chica (mediana, grande, extra-grande, 2X-grande) Las Instrucciones se muestran para talla chica, las demás tallas en paréntesis. Cuando solo se indique un número, aplica para todas las tallas.

Medidas finales

Pecho: 41 (44, 48, 54, 60) pulgadas

Materiales

- Estambre Patons Carmen voluminoso (1.75 oz/64 yds/50g por madeja): 9 (10, 11, 12, 13) madejas camel #07010
- Agujas para tejer número 10½ (6.5mm)
- Agujas para tejer número 11 (8mm) o medir para obtener la muestra del punto
- 2 marcadores de plástico
- Broche de flor comprado (opcional)
- Juego de broche grande

5 ABULTADO

Muestra de punto

12 pts y 14 hileras = 4 pulgadas/10 cm en p.jer
Comprobar la muestra del punto.

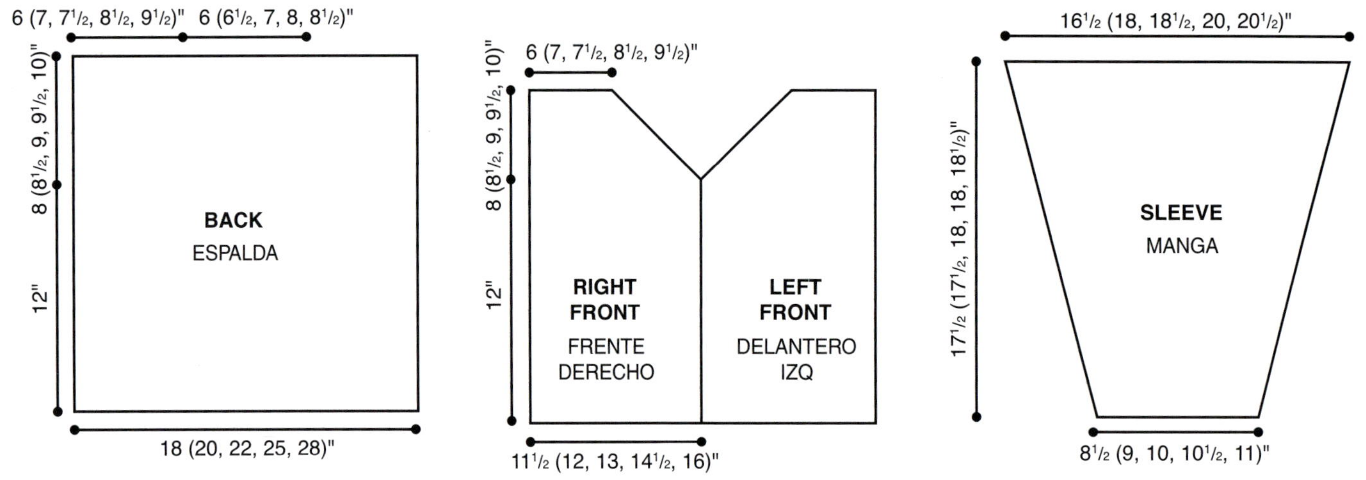

Back

***Note:** Knit fabric will be loose and stretchy which makes for a close-to-the–body fit that has plenty of give and is most comfortable. However, you will find that as you knit, sts tend to move closer to one another. When measuring, be careful to lay out the piece and smooth out evenly until it is flat.*

With larger needle, cast on 56 (62, 68, 76, 84) sts.

Row 1 (WS): Purl.

Row 2 (RS): Knit.

Rep Rows 1 and 2 until piece measures 20 (20½, 21, 21½, 22) inches, ending with a WS row.

Bind off 19 (21, 23, 26, 29) sts at beg of next 2 rows. (18, 20, 22, 24, 26 sts)

Bind off rem sts.

Right Front

With larger needle, cast on 35 (37, 40, 44, 48) sts.

Row 1 (WS): Purl.

Row 2 (RS): Knit.

Rep Rows 1 and 2 until piece measures 12 inches, ending with a WS row.

Shape neck

Row 1: K2tog, knit across.

***Note:** Place marker at beg of row to mark beg of V-neck shaping.*

Row 2: Purl to last 2 sts, p2tog.

Rep Rows 1 and 2 until 19 (21, 23, 26, 29) sts rem.

Work even in St st until piece measures 8 (8½, 9, 9½, 10) inches above marker, ending with a RS row.

Bind off.

Left Front

With larger needle, cast on 35 (37, 40, 44, 48) sts.

Row 1 (WS): Purl.

Row 2 (RS): Knit.

Rep Rows 1 and 2 until piece measures 12 inches, ending with a WS row.

Shape neck

Row 1 (RS): Knit to last 2 sts, k2tog.

***Note:** Place marker at end of row to mark beg of V-neck shaping.*

Row 2 (WS): P2tog, purl across.

Rows 1 and 2 until 19 (21, 23, 26, 29) sts rem. Work even in St st until piece measures 8 (8½, 9, 9½, 10) inches above marker, ending with WS row.

Bind off.

Espalda

***Nota:** El tejido quedará suelto y elástico, permitiendo un ajuste perfecto con suficiente holgura. Al medir, asegurarse de extender parejo el tejido.*

Con la aguja más grande, montar 56 (62, 68, 76, 84) pts.

Hilera 1 (LR): Revés.

Hilera 2 (LD): Derecho.

Rep Hileras 1 y 2 hasta que la pieza mida 20 (20½, 21, 21½, 22) pulgadas, terminando con una hilera LR.

Cerrar 19 (21, 23, 26, 29) pts al inic de sig 2 hileras. (18, 20, 22, 24, 26 pts)

Cerrar pts res.

Frente Derecho

Con la aguja más grande, montar 35 (37, 40, 44, 48) pts.

Hilera 1 (LR): Revés.

Hilera 2 (LD): Derecho.

Rep Hileras 1 y 2 hasta que la pieza mida 12 pulgadas, terminando con una hilera LR.

Formar cuello

Hilera 1: Der2jun, derecho a lo largo.

***Nota:** Coloque el marcador al inic de hilera para marcar inic de forma cuello-V.*

Hilera 2: Revés hasta últimos 2 pts, rev2jun.

Rep Hileras 1 y 2 hasta 19 (21, 23, 26, 29) pts res.

Trabajar uniformemente en p.jer hasta que la pieza mida 8 (8½, 9, 9½, 10) pulgadas arriba del marcador, terminando con una hilera LD.

Cerrar.

Delantero Izq

Con la aguja más grande, montar 35 (37, 40, 44, 48) pts.

Hilera 1 (LR): Revés.

Hilera 2 (LD): Derecho.

Rep Hileras 1 y 2 hasta que la pieza mida 12 pulgadas, terminando con una hilera LR.

Formar cuello

Hilera 1 (LD): Derecho hasta últimos 2 pts, der2jun.

***Nota:** Coloque el marcador al final de hilera para marcar inic de forma cuello-V.*

Hilera 2 (LR): Rev2jun, revés a lo largo.

Hileras 1 y 2 hasta 19 (21, 23, 26, 29) pts res. Trabajar uniformemente en p.jer hasta que la pieza mida 8 (8½, 9, 9½, 10) pulgadas arriba del marcador, terminando con hilera LR.

Cerrar.

Sleeves

With larger needle, cast on 26 (28, 30, 32, 34) sts.

Row 1 (WS): Purl.

Row 2 (RS): Knit.

Rep Rows 1 and 2 inc 1 st each edge [every 4th row] 12 (13, 13, 14, 14) times. (50, 54, 56, 60, 62 sts)

Continue even in St st until sleeve measures 17½ (17½, 18, 18, 18½) inches, ending with a WS row.

Bind off.

Finishing

Sew shoulder seams. Place markers 8 (8½, 9, 9½, 10) inches from shoulder seam along front and back armhole edge. Matching center of sleeve to shoulder seams and edges to markers, sew in sleeves. Sew side and sleeve in one continuous seam.

Collar

Row 1: Hold piece with RS of right front facing, with smaller needles, pick up and knit 29 (31, 33, 35, 37) sts from marker to shoulder seam, pick up and knit 18 (20, 22, 24, 26) sts across back neck, pick up and knit 29 (31, 33, 35, 37) sts from shoulder seam to marker. (76, 82, 88, 94, 100 sts)

Row 2: Purl.

Row 3: Sl 1k, k1, psso, k1, pass next st on RH needle over k1, knit to last st, sl last st knitwise.

Change to larger needles.

Row 4: Sl p1, p1, psso, p1, pass next st on RH needle over p1, purl to last st, sl last st purlwise.

With larger needles, [rep Rows 3 and 4] 7 (8, 9, 10, 11) times. (44, 46, 48, 50, 52 sts)

Knit 1 row even.

Purl 1 row even.

Bind off and weave in all ends.

Flower closure

Referring to photo, pin flower to Right Front. Sew on snap beneath flower.

Mangas

Con la aguja más grande, montar 26 (28, 30, 32, 34) pts.

Hilera 1 (LR): Revés.

Hilera 2 (LD): Derecho.

Rep Hileras 1 y 2 aum 1 pt cada orilla [cada 4a hilera] 12 (13, 13, 14, 14) veces. (50, 54, 56, 60, 62 pts)

Continuar uniformemente en p.jer hasta que manga mida 17½ (17½, 18, 18, 18½) pulgadas, terminando con una hilera LR.

Cerrar.

Acabado

Coser las costuras del hombro. Colocar marcadores a 8 (8½, 9, 9½, 10) pulgadas desde la costura del hombro a lo largo de la orilla de la sisa delantera y trasera. Coser mangas, igualando el centro de la manga a las costuras del hombro y las orillas a los marcadores. Coser costado y manga con una costura continua.

Escote

Hilera 1: Sostener la pieza viendo LD del frente derecho, con agujas más pequeñas, recoger y der 29 (31, 33, 35, 37) pts desde el marcador hasta la costura del hombro, recoger y der 18 (20, 22, 24, 26) pts a lo largo del cuello trasero, recoger y der 29 (31, 33, 35, 37) pts desde la costura del hombro hasta el marcador. (76, 82, 88, 94, 100 pts)

Hilera 2: Revés.

Hilera 3: Pst-d-p, der1, pasar sig pt sobre aguja MD sobre der1, der hasta último(s) pt, pst ult pt en sentido del tejido.

Cambiar a agujas grandes.

Hilera 4: Pst-r-p, rev1, pasar sig pt sobre aguja MD sobre rev1, rev hasta último(s) pt, pst ult pt en reverso del tejido.

Con agujas más grandes, [rep Hileras 3 y 4] 7 (8, 9, 10, 11) veces. (44, 46, 48, 50, 52 pts)

Der 1 hilera uniformemente.

Rev 1 hilera uniformemente.

Cerrar y entretejer todos los extremos sueltos.

Cierre con flor

Refiriéndose a la foto, prender flor al Frente Derecho. Coser con broche de presión abajo de la flor.

Go-Everywhere Jacket

Saco para Ir a Todas Partes

Skill Level

EASY

Sizes

Woman's small (medium, large, extra-large, 2X-large) Instructions are given for smallest size with larger sizes in parentheses. When only 1 number is given, it applies to all sizes.

Finished Measurements

Chest: 46 (50, 54, 58, 62) inches

Materials

- Lion Brand Lion Bouclé super bulky weight yarn (2.5 oz/57 yds/ 70g per ball): 9 (10, 11, 12, 13) balls wild berries #210 (A)
- Lion Brand Lion Suede bulky weight yarn (3 oz/122 yds/85g per ball): 1 ball denim #110 (B)
- Size 11 (8mm) knitting needles or size needed to obtain gauge
- Sizes G/6/4mm and J/10/6mm crochet hooks
- Yarn needle
- Stitch holder

6 SUPER BULKY

5 BULKY

Gauge

8 sts and 12 rows = 4 inches/10cm in St st
To save time, take time to check gauge.

Back

With A, cast on 40 (44, 48, 52, 56) sts.

Row 1 (WS): Purl.

Row 2 (RS): Knit.

Rep Rows 1 and 2 until piece measures 23 (23½, 24, 24½, 25) inches, ending with a WS row.

Nivel de dificultad

FÁCIL

Tallas

Dama chica (mediana, grande, extra-grande, 2X-grande) Las instrucciones se muestran para talla chica, las demás tallas en paréntesis. Cuando solo se indique un número, aplica para todas las tallas.

Medidas finales

Pecho: 46 (50, 54, 58, 62) pulgadas

Materiales

- Estambre Lion Brand Lion Bouclé super voluminoso (2.5 oz/57 yds/ 70g por bola): 9 (10, 11, 12, 13) bolas wild berries #210 (A)
- Estambre Lion Brand Lion Suede voluminoso (3 oz/122 yds/ 85g por bola): 1 bola denim #110 (B)
- Agujas para tejer número 11 (8mm) o medir para obtener la muestra del punto
- Ganchos de tejer números G/6/4mm y J/10/6mm
- Aguja gruesa para coser estambre
- Sujeta puntos

6 SÚPER ABULTADO

5 ABULTADO

Muestra de punto

8 pts y 12 hileras = 4 pulgadas/10cm en p.jer
Comprobar la muestra del punto.

Espalda

Con A, montar 40 (44, 48, 52, 56) pts.

Hilera 1 (LR): Revés.

Hilera 2 (LD): Derecho.

Rep Hileras 1 y 2 hasta que la pieza mida 23 (23½, 24, 24½, 25) pulgadas, terminando con una hilera LR.

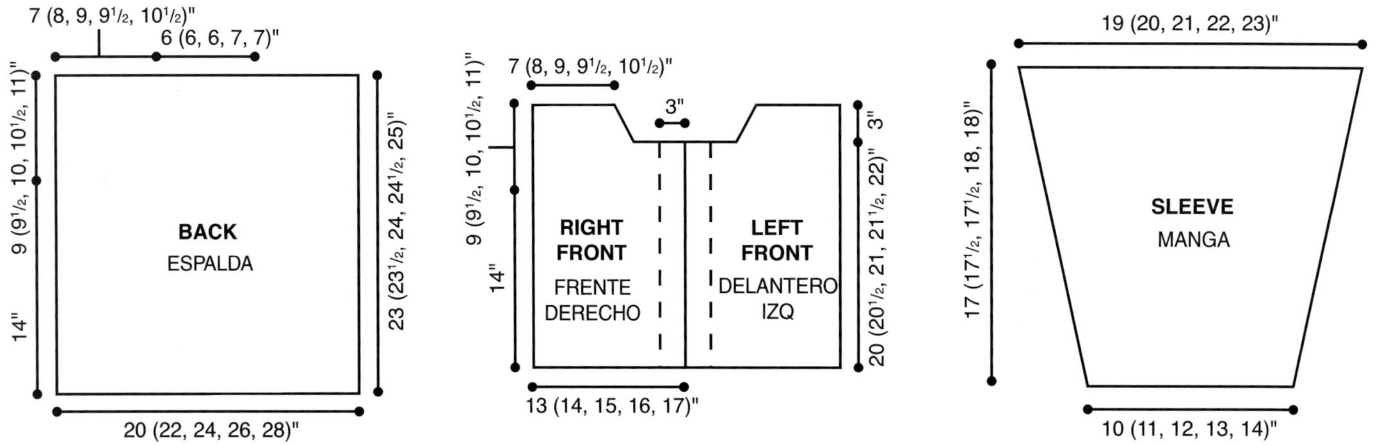

Bind off 14 (16, 18, 19, 21) sts at beg of next 2 rows.
Sl rem 12 (12, 12, 14, 14) sts onto st holder.

Cerrar 14 (16, 18, 19, 21) pts al inic de sig 2 hileras.
Pst rest 12 (12, 12, 14, 14) pts al sujeta puntos.

Right Front

With A, cast on 26 (28, 30, 32, 34) sts.

Row 1 (WS): Purl.

Row 2 (RS): Knit.

Rep Rows 1 and 2 until piece measures 20 (20½, 21, 21½, 22) inches, ending with WS row.

Frente Derecho

Con A, montar 26 (28, 30, 32, 34) pts.

Hilera 1 (LR): Revés.

Hilera 2 (LD): Derecho.

Rep Hileras 1 y 2 hasta que la pieza mida 20 (20½, 21, 21½, 22) pulgadas, terminando con hilera LR.

Shape Neck

Row 1: Bind off 9 (9, 9, 10, 10) sts, knit across. (17, 19, 21, 22, 24 sts)

Row 2: Purl.

Row 3: K2 tog, knit across.

Row 4: Purl.

Rows 5–8: [Rep Rows 3 and 4] twice. (14, 16, 18, 19, 21 sts)

Bind off.

Formar cuello

Hilera 1: Cerrar 9 (9, 9, 10, 10) pts, der a lo largo. (17, 19, 21, 22, 24 pts)

Hilera 2: Revés.

Hilera 3: Der2jun, derecho a lo largo.

Hilera 4: Revés.

Hileras 5-8: [Rep Hileras 3 y 4] 2 veces. (14, 16, 18, 19, 21 pts)

Cerrar.

Left Front

With A, cast on 26 (28, 30, 32, 34) sts.

Row 1 (WS): Purl.

Row 2 (RS): Knit.

Rep Rows 1 and 2 until same length as right front to neck shaping, ending with RS row.

Delantero Izq

Con A, montar 26 (28, 30, 32, 34) pts.

Hilera 1 (LR): Revés.

Hilera 2 (LD): Derecho.

Rep Hileras 1 y 2 hasta la misma longitud que delantero der hasta base del cuello, terminando con hilera LD.

Shape Neck

Row 1 (WS): Bind off 9 (9, 9, 10, 10) sts, purl across. (17, 19, 21, 22, 24 sts)

Row 2 (RS): Knit.

Row 3: K2 tog, purl across.

Row 4: Knit.

Row 5–8: [Rep Rows 3 and 4] twice. (14, 16, 18, 19, 21 sts)

Bind off.

Formar cuello

Hilera 1 (LR): Cerrar 9 (9, 9, 10, 10) pts revés a lo largo. (17, 19, 21 22, 24 pts)

Hilera 2 (LD): Derecho.

Hilera 3: Der2jun, rev a lo largo.

Hilera 4: Derecho.

Hileras 5-8: [Rep Hileras 3 y 4] 2 veces. (14, 16, 18, 19, 21 pts)

Cerrar.

Sleeves

With A, cast on 20 (22, 24, 26, 28) sts.

Row 1 (WS): Purl.

Row 2 (RS): Knit.

Row 3: Purl.

Row 4: Inc, knit to last st, inc.

[Rep Rows 1–4] 8 times. (38, 40, 42, 44, 46 sts)

Work even in St st until sleeve measures 17 (17½, 17½, 18, 18) inches.

Bind off.

Mangas

Con A, montar 20 (22, 24, 26, 28) pts.

Hilera 1 (LR): Revés.

Hilera 2 (LD): Derecho.

Hilera 3: Revés.

Hilera 4: Aum, der hasta último pt, aum.

[Rep Hileras 1–4] 8 veces. (38, 40, 42, 44, 46 pts)

Trabajar uniformemente en p.jer hasta que la manga mida 17 (17½, 17½, 18, 18) pulgadas.

Cerrar.

Assembly

Sew shoulder seams. Place markers 9 (9½, 10, 10½, 11) inches from shoulder seam along front and back armhole edge. Sew sleeve between markers. Sew sleeve and side in continuous seam.

Button

Note: *If not familiar with crochet chain (ch) and single crochet (sc) sts refer to crochet Stitch Guide on page 38.*

With smaller crochet hook and B, ch 2, 12 sc in 2nd ch from hook.

Fasten off, leaving long tail.

Thread tail into yarn needle and weave through top lps of sc, pull tightly and sew securely on WS.

Edgings

Sleeve edging

With RS facing, smaller crochet hook and A, attach yarn with sl st at one sleeve seam. Sc in each st around lower edge.

Join and fasten off.

Rep on other sleeve.

Front & lower edging

With RS of left front facing, larger crochet hook and A, attach yarn with sl st at end of bound off sts, ch 1, sc along neck edge to corner, 3 sc in corner, sc in along left front to next corner, 3 sc in corner, sc across bottom edge to next corner, 3 sc in corner, sc along right front to 1 inch from neck edge, ch 5 for buttonhole, 3 sc in corner, sc across bound off sts along neck edge.

Fasten off.

Collar

Row 1 (RS): With RS of right front facing, larger crochet hook and B, join in 6th st from center front, work 43 (45, 47, 49, 51) sc around neck leaving 5 sts unworked at left center front. Turn.

Rows 2–5: Ch 1, sc in each sc. Turn.

Fasten off.

Finishing

Referring to photo for placement, sew button to left front opposite button lp.

Ensamblar

Coser las costuras del hombro. Colocar marcadores a 9 (9½, 10, 10½, 11) pulgadas desde la costura del hombro a lo largo de la orilla de la sisa delantera y trasera. Coser manga entre marcadores. Coser manga y costado con una costura continua.

Botón

Nota: *Referirse a la Guía de Puntos de crochet en la página 39.*

Con gancho para tejer más pequeño y B, cad 2, 12 cs en 2a cad desde el gancho.

Rematar, dejando cadena larga.

Enhebre la cadena en la aguja para coser gruesa y entreteja a través de las lazadas de cs, jale fuertemente y cosa firmemente en LR.

Orillas

Orillas de la Manga

Viendo LD, con gancho de tejer más pequeño y A, unir estambre con pst en una costura de la manga. Cs en cada pt alrededor de la orilla inferior.

Unir y rematar.

Rep en otra manga.

Orillas del frente e inferior

Con LD del frente izq, gancho de tejer grande y A, unir estambre con pst al final de pts sueltos, cad1, cs a lo largo de orilla del cuello hasta la esquina, 3 cs en esquina, cs a lo largo de frente izq hasta sig esquina, 3 cs en esquina, cs a través de orilla inferior hasta sig esquina, 3 cs en esquina, cs a lo largo de frente der hasta 1 pulgada desde orilla cuello, cad5 para ojal. 3 cs en esquina, cs a través pts sueltos a lo largo orilla cuello.

Rematar.

Escote

Hilera 1 (LD): Con LD del frente der, gancho de tejer grande y B, unir en 6°. pt desde el centro del frente, trabajar 43 (45, 47, 49, 51) cs alrededor del cuello, dejando 5 pts sin trabajar al centro izq del frente. Vuelta.

Hileras 2-5: Cad 1, cs en cada cs. Vuelta.

Rematar.

Acabado

Refiriéndose a fotografía, coser botón en el frente izq, del otro lado de ojal.

Be-Ribboned Shrug

Chaqueta Encintada

Skill Level

EASY

Sizes

Woman's small (medium, large, extra-large, 2X-large) Instructions are given for smallest size, with larger sizes in parentheses. When only 1 number is given, it applies to all sizes.

Finished Measurements

Chest: 36 (40, 44, 48, 52) inches

Materials

5 BULKY

- Moda Dea Prima bulky weight yarn (1.76 oz/72 yds/ 50g per ball): 5 (6, 6, 8, 9) balls natural #3259
- Size 9 (5.5mm) knitting needles
- Sizes 11 (8mm) knitting needles or size needed to obtain gauge
- Size J/10/6mm crochet hook
- 2 yds (1½-inch-wide) matching satin ribbon
- Sewing needle and matching thread

Gauge

12 sts and 16 rows = 4 inches/10cm in St st on larger needles

To save time, take time to check gauge.

Nivel de dificultad

FÁCIL

Tallas

Dama chica (mediana, grande, extra-grande, 2X-grande) Las Instrucciones se muestran para talla chica, las demás tallas en paréntesis. Cuando solo se indique un número, aplica para todas las tallas.

Medidas finales

Pecho: 36 (40, 44, 48, 52) pulgadas

Materiales

5 ABULTADO

- Estambre Moda Dea Prima voluminoso (1.76 oz/72 yds/50g por bola): 5 (6, 6, 8, 9) bolas natural #3259
- Agujas para tejer número 9 (5.5mm)
- Agujas para tejer número 11 (8mm) o medir para obtener la muestra del punto
- Gancho de tejer número J/10/6mm
- 2 yds (ancho 1½-pulgadas) listón satinado haciendo juego
- Aguja para coser e hilo haciendo juego

Muestra de punto

12 pts y 16 hileras = 4 pulgadas/10cm en p.jer con agujas más grandes

Comprobar la muestra del punto.

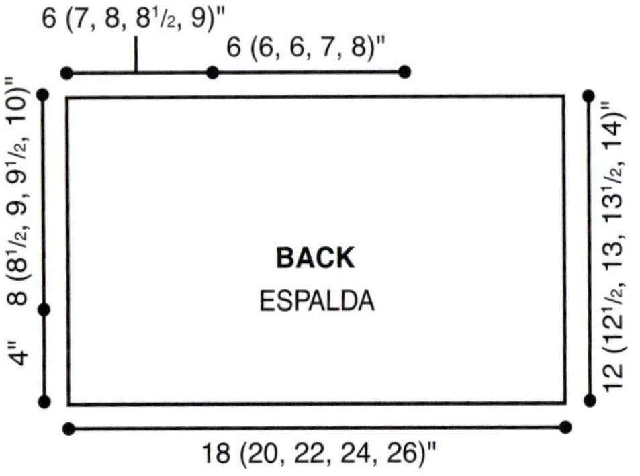

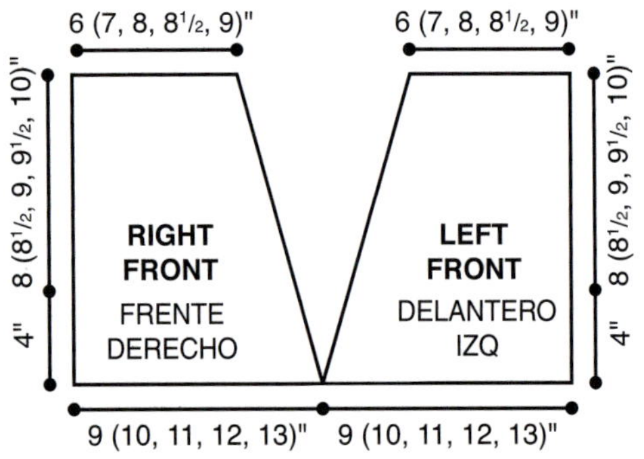

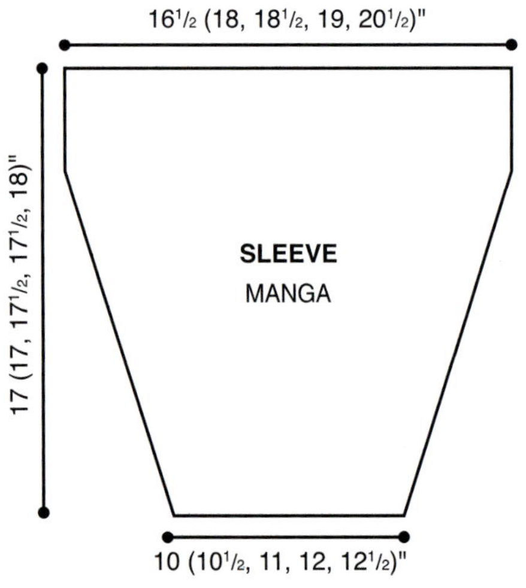

Back

With smaller needles, cast on 56 (62, 68, 74, 80) sts.

Ribbing

Row 1 (RS): *K1, p1; rep from * across.

Rows 2–6: Rep Row 1.

Change to larger needles.

Body

Row 1 (RS): Knit.

Row 2: Purl.

Rep Rows 1 and 2 until back measures 12 (12½, 13, 13½, 14) inches, ending with a WS row.

Bind off 19 (21, 23, 25, 27) sts at the beg of next 2 rows. (18, 20, 22, 24, 26 sts)

Bind off rem sts.

Right Front

With smaller needles, cast on 28 (30, 34, 36, 40) sts.

Ribbing

Row 1 (RS): *K1, p1; rep from * across.

Rows 2–5: Rep Row 1.

Row 6: Inc 0 (1, 0, 1, 0), work in pat as established across. (28, 31, 34, 37, 40 sts)

Change to larger needles.

Shape body & neck

Row 1 (RS): Knit.

Row 2: Purl.

Row 3: K1, ssk, knit across.

Row 4: Purl.

[Rep Rows 1–4] 8 (9, 9, 9, 10) times. (19, 21, 24, 26, 29 sts)

Work even until piece measures same as Back.

Bind off.

Left Front

With smaller needles, cast on 28 (30, 34, 36, 40) sts.

Ribbing

Row 1 (RS): *K1, p1; rep from * across.

Rows 2–5: Rep Row 1.

Row 6: Work in pat to last st, inc 0 (1, 0, 1, 0). (28, 31, 34, 37, 40 sts)

Change to larger needles.

Espalda

Con las agujas más chicas, montar 56 (62, 68, 74, 80) pts.

Cordoncillo

Hilera 1 (LD): *Der1, rev1; rep desde * a lo largo.

Hileras 2-6: Rep Hilera 1.

Cambiar a agujas grandes.

Cuerpo

Hilera 1 (LD): Derecho.

Hilera 2: Revés.

Rep Hileras 1 y 2 hasta que la espalda mida 12 (12½, 13, 13½, 14) pulgadas, terminando con una hilera LR.

Cerrar 19 (21, 23, 25, 27) pts al inic de sig 2 hileras. (18, 20, 22, 24, 26 pts)

Cerrar pts res.

Frente Derecho

Con las agujas más chicas, montar 28 (30, 34, 36, 40) pts.

Cordoncillo

Hilera 1 (LD): *Der1, rev1; rep desde * a lo largo.

Hileras 2-5: Rep Hilera 1.

Hilera 6: Aum 0 (1, 0, 1, 0), trabajar puntada a lo largo. (28, 31, 34, 37, 40 pts)

Cambiar a agujas grandes.

Formar cuerpo y cuello

Hilera 1 (LD): Derecho.

Hilera 2: Revés.

Hilera 3: Der1, pst-pst-der, der a lo largo.

Hilera 4: Revés.

[Rep Hileras 1–4] 8 (9, 9, 9, 10) veces. (19, 21, 24, 26, 29 pts)

Trabajar uniformemente hasta que la pieza mida lo mismo que la espalda.

Cerrar.

Delantero Izq

Con las agujas más chicas, montar 28 (30, 34, 36, 40) pts.

Cordoncillo

Hilera 1 (LD): *Der1, rev1; rep desde * a lo largo.

Hileras 2-5: Rep Hilera 1.

Hilera 6: Trabajar puntada hasta ult pt, aum 0 (1, 0, 1, 0). (28, 31, 34, 37, 40 pts)

Cambiar a agujas grandes.

Shape body & neck

Row 1 (RS): Knit.

Row 2: Purl.

Row 3: Knit to last 3 sts, k2tog, k1.

Row 4: Purl.

[Rep Rows 1–4] 8 (9, 9, 9, 10) times. (19, 21, 24, 26, 29 sts)

Work even until piece measures same as Back.

Bind off.

Sleeves

With smaller needles cast on 30 (32, 34, 36, 38) sts.

Ribbing

Row 1 (RS): *K1, p1; rep from * across.

Rows 2–10: Rep Row 1.

Change to larger needles.

Body

Row 1 (RS): Knit.

Row 2: Purl.

Row 3: Inc, knit to last st, inc.

Row 4: Purl.

[Rep Rows 1–4] 9 (11, 11, 12, 13) times. (50, 56, 58, 62, 66 sts)

Work even until sleeve measures 17 (17, 17½, 17½, 18) inches.

Bind off all sts.

Assembly

Sew shoulder seams. Place markers 8 (8½, 9, 9½, 10) from shoulder seam along front and back armhole edge. Matching center of sleeve to shoulder seam and edges to markers, sew in sleeves. Sew side and sleeve in continuous seam.

Front edging

Note: *If not familiar with single crochet (sc) st refer to crochet Stitch Guide on page 38.*

Hold with RS of right front facing, with crochet hook, sc along right front, neck, and Left Front.

Fasten off.

Ties & Bows

Cut ribbon into 4 (18-inch) lengths. Tie 2 lengths into bows and referring to photo sew to lower sleeves. Sew rem 2 lengths to lower front for ties.

Formar cuerpo y cuello

Hilera 1 (LD): Derecho.

Hilera 2: Revés.

Hilera 3: Derecho hasta últimos 3 pts, der2jun, der1.

Hilera 4: Revés.

[Rep Hileras 1–4] 8 (9, 9, 9, 10) veces. (19, 21, 24, 26, 29 pts)

Trabajar uniformemente hasta que la pieza mida lo mismo que la espalda.

Cerrar.

Mangas

Con agujas más pequeñas, montar 30 (32, 34, 36, 38) pts.

Cordoncillo

Hilera 1 (LD): *Der1, rev1; rep desde * a lo largo.

Hileras 2-10: Rep Hilera 1.

Cambiar a agujas grandes.

Cuerpo

Hilera 1 (LD): Derecho.

Hilera 2: Revés.

Hilera 3: Aum, der hasta último pt, aum.

Hilera 4: Revés.

[Rep Hileras 1–4] 9 (11, 11, 12, 13) veces. (50, 56, 58, 62, 66 pts)

Trabajar uniformemente hasta que la manga mida 17 (17, 17½, 17½, 18) pulgadas.

Cerrar todos los pts.

Ensamblar

Coser las costuras del hombro. Colocar marcadores a 8 (8½, 9, 9½, 10) pulgadas desde la costura del hombro a lo largo de la orilla de la sisa delantera y trasera. Coser mangas, igualando el centro de la manga a la costura del hombro y las orillas a los marcadores. Coser costado y manga con una costura continua.

Orillas del Frente

Nota: *Referirse a la Guía de Puntos de crochet en la página 39.*

Sostener con LD del frente der, con gancho de tejer, cs a lo largo de frente der, cuello y frente izq.

Rematar.

Corbatas y Moños

Cortar listón en 4 tramos de (18-pulgadas). Amarrar 2 tramos en moños y coser en parte inferior de las mangas como en la fotografía. Coser rest 2 tramos en frente inferior como corbatas.

Comfy Little Topper

Skill Level

EASY

Sizes

Woman's small (medium, large, extra-large, 2X-large) Instructions are given for smallest size, with larger sizes in parentheses. When only 1 number is given, it applies to all sizes.

Finished Measurements

Chest: 36 (40, 44, 48, 52) inches

Materials

- Bernat Eye Lash super bulky weight yarn (1.75 oz/77 yds/50g per ball): 3 (4, 5, 6, 7) balls flash #35315 (A) — 6 SUPER BULKY
- Bernat Bling Bling bulky weight yarn (1.75 oz/90 yds/50g per ball): 1 ball sassy sparkle #65208 (B) — 5 BULKY
- Size 10½ (6.5mm) knitting needles
- Size 11 (8mm) knitting needles or size needed to obtain gauge
- Size G/6/4mm crochet hook

Gauge

12 sts and 16 rows = 4 inches/10 cm in St st on larger needles

To save time, take time to check gauge.

Back

With smaller needles and B, cast on 54 (60, 66, 72, 78) sts.

Row 1 (WS): Purl.

Row 2 (RS): Knit.

Row 3: Purl.

Change to larger needles and A.

Row 4: Knit.

Continue in St st with A until back measures 5 inches.

Pequeño Top Cómodo

Nivel de dificultad

FÁCIL

Tallas

Dama chica (mediana, grande, extra-grande, 2X-grande) Las instrucciones se muestran para talla chica, las demás tallas en paréntesis. Cuando sólo se indique un número, aplica para todas las tallas.

Medidas finales

Pecho: 36 (40, 44, 48, 52) pulgadas

Materiales

- Estambre Bernat Eye Lash super voluminoso (1.75 oz/77 yds/50g por bola): 3 (4, 5, 6, 7) bolas flash #35315 (A) — 6 SÚPER ABULTADO
- Estambre Bernat Bling Bling voluminoso (1.75 oz/90 yds/50g por bola): 1 bola sassy sparkle #65208 (B) — 5 ABULTADO
- Agujas para tejer número 10½ (6.5mm)
- Agujas para tejer número 11 (8mm) o medir para obtener la muestra del punto
- Gancho de tejer número G/6/4mm

Muestra de punto

12 pts y 16 hileras = 4 pulgadas/10 cm en p.jer con agujas más grandes

Comprobar la muestra del punto.

Espalda

Con las agujas más chicas y B, montar 54 (60, 66, 72, 78) pts.

Hilera 1 (LR): Revés.

Hilera 2 (LD): Derecho.

Hilera 3: Revés.

Cambiar a agujas grandes y A.

Hilera 4: Derecho.

Continuar con p.jer con A hasta que la espalda mida 5 pulgadas.

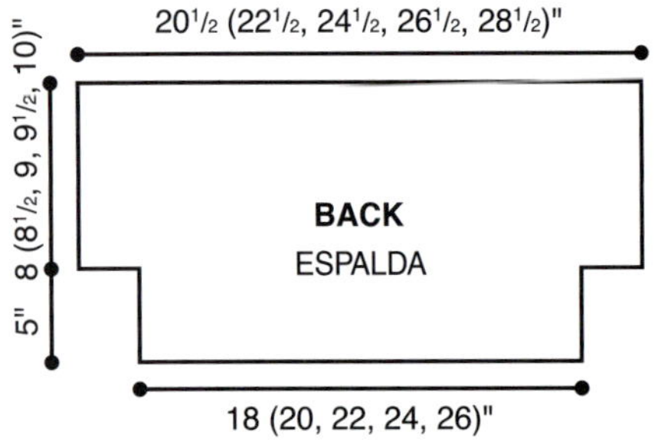

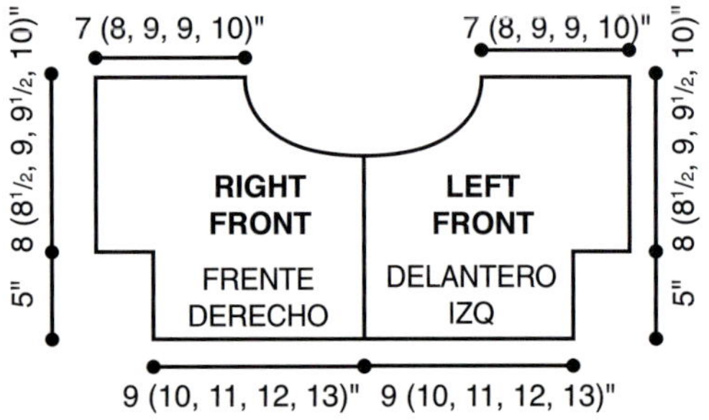

Sleeves

Cast on 4 sts at the beg of next 2 rows. (62, 68, 74, 80, 86 sts)

Continue even in St st until sleeve measures 8 (8½, 9, 9½, 10) inches.

Bind off 22 (24, 27, 29, 31) sts at beg of next 2 rows. (18, 20, 20, 22, 24 sts)

Bind off rem sts.

Right Front

With smaller needles and B, cast on 27 (30, 33, 36, 39) sts.

Row 1 (WS): Purl.

Row 2 (RS): Knit.

Row 3: Purl.

Change to larger needles and A.

Mangas

Montar 4 pts al inic de sig 2 hileras. (62, 68, 74, 80, 86 pts)

Continuar uniformemente en p.jer hasta que la manga mida 8 (8½, 9, 9½, 10) pulgadas.

Cerrar 22 (24, 27, 29, 31) pts al inic de sig 2 hileras. (18, 20, 20, 22, 24 pts)

Cerrar pts res.

Frente Derecho

Con las agujas más chicas y B, montar 27 (30, 33, 36, 39) pts.

Hilera 1 (LR): Revés.

Hilera 2 (LD): Derecho.

Hilera 3: Revés.

Cambiar a agujas grandes y A.

Row 4: Knit.

Continue in St st until right front measures 5 inches, ending with a RS row.

Sleeve

Cast on 4 sts, purl across. (31, 34, 37, 40, 43 sts)
Continue to work in St st until sleeve measures 4½ (5, 5½, 6, 6½) inches, ending with WS row.

Shape neck

Row 1 (RS): Bind off 6 (7, 7, 8, 9) sts, knit across. (25, 27, 30, 32, 34 sts)

Row 2: Purl.

Row 3: K2 tog, knit across.

Rows 4–7: [Rep Rows 2 and 3] twice. (22, 24, 27, 29, 31 sts)

Work even in St st until sleeve measures 8 (8½, 9, 9½, 10) inches.

Bind off all sts.

Left Front

With smaller needles and B, cast on 27 (30, 33, 36, 39) sts.

Row 1 (WS): Purl.

Row 2 (RS): Knit.

Row 3: Purl.

Change to larger needles and A.

Row 4: Knit.

Continue in St st until left front measures 5 inches, ending with a RS row.

Cast on 4 sts, purl across. (31, 34, 37, 40, 43 sts)

Continue even in St st until sleeve measures 4½ (5, 5½, 6, 6 ½) inches, ending with a RS row.

Shape neck

Row 1 (WS): Bind off 6 (7, 7, 8, 9) sts, purl across. (25, 27, 30, 32, 34 sts)

Row 2 (RS): Knit.

Row 3: Purl to last 2 sts, p2 tog.

Rows 4–7: [Rep Rows 2 and 3] twice. (22, 24, 27, 29, 31 sts)

Continue even in St st until sleeve measures 8 (8½, 9, 9½, 10) inches, ending with RS row.

Bind off all sts.

Assemble

Sew side/sleeve seam.

Hilera 4: Derecho.

Continuar en p.jer hasta que el frente der mida 5 pulgadas, terminando con una hilera LD.

Manga

Montar 4 pts, rev a lo largo. (31, 34, 37, 40, 43 pts)
Continuar trabajando en p.jer hasta que la manga mida 4½ (5, 5½, 6, 6½) pulgadas, terminando con una hilera LR.

Formar cuello

Hilera 1 (LD): Cerrar 6 (7, 7, 8, 9) pts der a lo largo. (25, 27, 30, 32, 34 pts)

Hilera 2: Revés.

Hilera 3: Der2jun, derecho a lo largo.

Hileras 4-7: [Rep Hileras 2 y 3] 2 veces. (22, 24, 27, 29, 31 pts)

Continuar uniformemente en p.jer hasta que la manga mida 8 (8½, 9, 9½, 10) pulgadas.

Cerrar todos los pts.

Delantero Izq

Con las agujas más chicas y B, montar 27 (30, 33, 36, 39) pts.

Hilera 1 (LR): Revés.

Hilera 2 (LD): Derecho.

Hilera 3: Revés.

Cambiar a agujas grandes y A.

Hilera 4: Derecho.

Continuar en p.jer hasta que el frente izq mida 5 pulgadas, terminando con una hilera LD.

Montar 4 pts, rev a lo largo. (31, 34, 37, 40, 43 pts)

Continuar uniformemente en p.jer hasta que manga mida 4½ (5, 5½, 6, 6 ½) pulgadas, terminando con una hilera LD.

Formar cuello

Hilera 1 (LR): Cerrar 6 (7, 7, 8, 9) pts revés a lo largo. (25, 27, 30, 32, 34 pts)

Hilera 2 (LD): Derecho.

Hilera 3: Revés hasta últimos 2 pts, rev2jun.

Hileras 4-7: [Rep Hileras 2 y 3] 2 veces. (22, 24, 27, 29, 31 pts)

Continuar uniformemente en p.jer hasta que la manga mida 8 (8½, 9, 9½, 10) pulgadas, terminando con una hilera LD.

Cerrar todos los pts.

Ensamblar

Coser las costuras laterales y de la manga.

Sleeve Edging

Row 1 (RS): Hold 1 sleeve with RS facing, with smaller needles and B, pick up and knit 46 (48, 50, 52, 54) sts evenly spaced along sleeve edge.

Row 2: Purl.

Row 3: Knit.

Row 4: Purl.

Bind off all sts.

Rep on other sleeve.

Right Front Band

Row 1: Hold with RS of right front facing, with smaller needles and B, pick up and knit 35 (37, 39, 41, 43) sts evenly spaced along center front edge.

Row 2: Purl.

Row 3: Knit.

Row 4: Purl.

Bind off all sts.

Left Front Band

Row 1: Hold with RS of left front facing, with smaller needles and B, pick up and knit 35 (37, 39, 41, 43) sts evenly spaced along center front edge.

Row 2: Purl.

Row 3: Knit.

Row 4: Purl.

Bind off all sts

Neck Band

Row 1: Hold with RS facing, with smaller needles and B, pick up and knit 22 (24, 26, 28, 30) sts from center right front to right shoulder, pick up and knit 18 (20, 20, 22, 24) sts across back neck, pick up and knit 22 (24, 26, 28, 30) sts from left shoulder to center left front. (62, 68, 72, 78, 84 sts)

Row 2: Purl.

Row 3: Knit.

Row 4: Purl.

Bind off all sts.

Tie

For each tie, cut 1 (3-yd) length of B and fold in half. Join folded length at upper neck edge of 1 front, chain to end. Fasten off. Rep on other front.

Orillas de la Manga

Hilera 1 (LD): Sostener 1 manga viendo LD, con agujas más pequeñas y B, recoger y der 46 (48, 50, 52, 54) pts espaciados uniformemente a lo largo de la orilla de la manga.

Hilera 2: Revés.

Hilera 3: Derecho.

Hilera 4: Revés.

Cerrar todos los pts.

Rep en otra manga.

Cinta Delantera Derecha

Hilera 1: Sostener frente der viendo LD, con agujas más pequeñas y B, recoger y der 35 (37, 39, 41, 43) pts espaciados uniformemente a lo largo de la orilla del centro delantero.

Hilera 2: Revés.

Hilera 3: Derecho.

Hilera 4: Revés.

Cerrar todos los pts.

Cinta Delantera Izquierda

Hilera 1: Sostener frente izq viendo LD, con agujas más pequeñas y B, recoger y der 35 (37, 39, 41, 43) pts espaciados uniformemente a lo largo de la orilla del centro delantero.

Hilera 2: Revés.

Hilera 3: Derecho.

Hilera 4: Revés.

Cerrar todos los pts.

Cinta del Cuello

Hilera 1: Sostener viendo LD, con agujas más pequeñas y B, recoger y der 22 (24, 26, 28, 30) pts centro delantero der con hombro der, recoger y der 18 (20, 20, 22, 24) pts a lo largo del cuello trasero, recoger y der 22 (24, 26, 28, 30) pts desde el hombro izq hasta el frente del centro izq. (62, 68, 72, 78, 84 pts)

Hilera 2: Revés.

Hilera 3: Derecho.

Hilera 4: Revés.

Cerrar todos los pts.

Corbata

Para cada corbata, cortar 1 tramo (3-yd) de B y doblar a la mitad. Unir el tramo doblado en la orilla superior del cuello de un frente, unir en cadena hasta el final. Rematar. Rep en el otro frente.

Fur-Collar Cardi

Chaqueta de Punto con Cuello de Piel

Skill Level

EASY

Sizes

Woman's small (medium, large, extra-large, 2X-large) Instructions are given for smallest size, with larger sizes in parentheses. When only 1 number is given, it applies to all sizes.

Finished Measurements

Chest: 36 (40, 44, 48, 52) inches

Materials

4 MEDIUM

5 BULKY

- TLC Amore medium weight yarn (6 oz/278 yds/170g per ball): 2 (3, 3, 4, 4) balls red velvet #3907 (A)
- Moda Dea Aerie bulky weight yarn (1.76 oz/68 yds/50g per ball): 1 (2, 2, 3, 3) balls red #9390 (B)
- Size 9 (5.5mm) straight and 24-inch circular knitting needles
- Sizes 11 (8mm) straight and 24-inch circular knitting needles or size needed to obtain gauge
- 2 size 8 (5mm) double-pointed needles
- Stitch markers
- 2 (3-inch-long) purchased decorative tassels

Gauge

12 sts and 18 rows = 4 inches/10cm in St st on larger needles

To save time, take time to check gauge.

Nivel de dificultad

FÁCIL

Tallas

Dama chica (mediana, grande, extra-grande, 2X-grande) Las instrucciones se muestran para talla chica, las demás tallas en paréntesis. Cuando sólo se indique un número, aplica para todas las tallas.

Medidas finales

Pecho: 36 (40, 44, 48, 52) pulgadas

Materiales

4 MEDIO

5 ABULTADO

- Estambre TLC Amore mediano (6 oz/278 yds/170g por bola): 2 (3, 3, 4, 4) bolas red velvet #3907 (A)
- Estambre Moda Dea Aerie voluminoso (1.76 oz/68 yds/50g por bola): 1 (2, 2, 3, 3) bolas red #9390 (B)
- Agujas para tejer rectas del número 9 (5.5mm) y circulares de 24-pulgadas
- Agujas para tejer rectas del número 11 (8mm) y circulares de 24-pulgadas o medir para obtener la muestra del punto
- 2 agujas de doble punta número 8 (5mm)
- Marcadores de anillo dividido
- 2 borlas decorativas (3-pulgadas de largo)

Muestra de punto

12 pts y 18 hileras = 4 pulgadas/10cm en p.jer con agujas más grandes

Comprobar la muestra del punto.

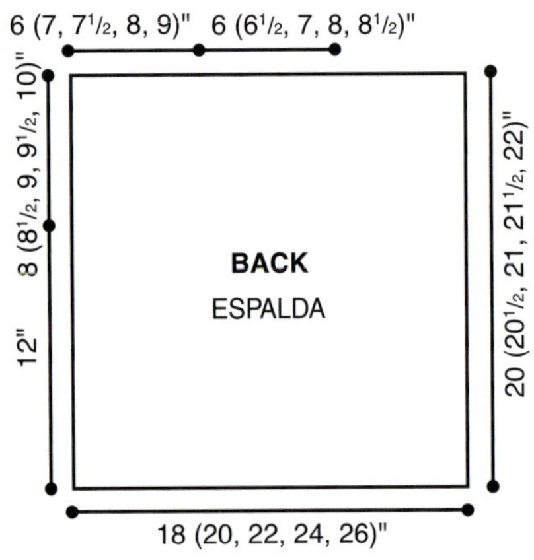

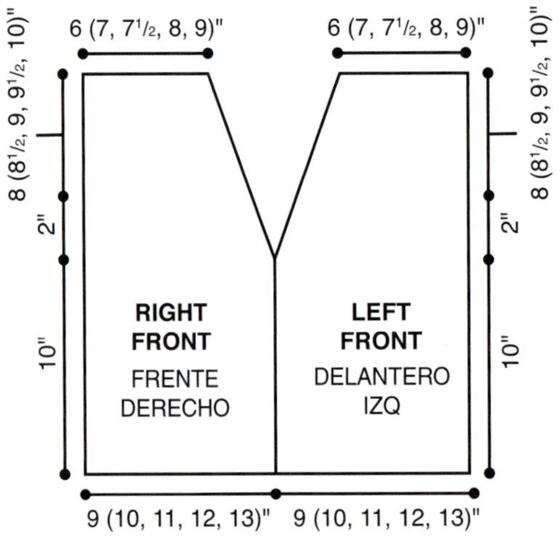

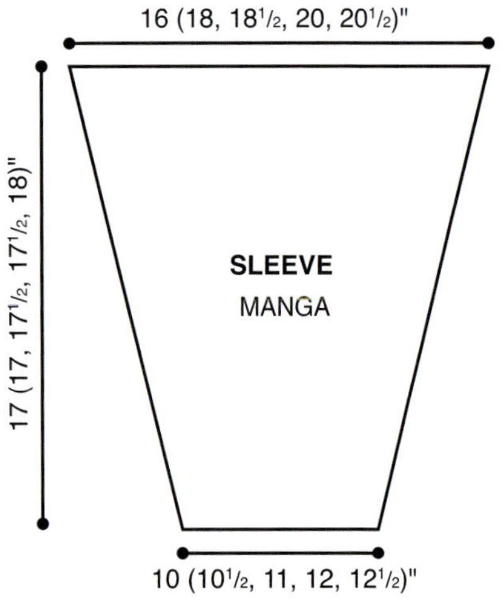

Back

With smaller straight needles and A, cast on 56 (62, 68, 74, 80) sts.

Row 1: *K1, p1; rep from * across.

Rows 2–4: Rep Row 1.

Change to larger needles.

Espalda

Con las agujas rectas más chicas y A, montar 56 (62, 68, 74, 80) pts.

Hilera 1: *Der1, rev1; rep desde * a lo largo.

Hileras 2-4: Rep Hilera 1.

Cambiar a agujas grandes.

Row 5: Knit.

Row 6: Purl.

Rep Rows 5 and 6 until piece measures 20 (20½, 21, 21½, 22) inches.

Bind off 19 (21, 23, 25, 27) sts at beg of next 2 rows. (18, 20, 22, 24, 26 sts)

Bind off rem sts.

Right Front

With smaller straight needles and A, cast on 28 (30, 34, 36, 40) sts.

Row 1 (RS): *K1, p1, rep from * across.

Rows 2 and 3: Rep Row 1.

Row 4: Inc 0 (1, 0, 1, 0), work in pat across. (28, 31, 34, 37, 40 sts)

Change to larger straight needles.

Row 5: Knit.

Row 6: Purl.

Rep Rows 5 and 6 until piece measures 10 inches, ending with WS row.

Shape neck

Row 1 (RS): K1, ssk, knit to end. (27, 30, 33, 36, 39 sts)

Row 2: Purl.

Continue in St st, dec 1 st at neck edge [every 6th row] 8 (9, 10, 11, 12) times. (19, 21, 23, 25, 27 sts)

Work even until piece measures 20 (20½, 21, 21½, 22) inches.

Bind off.

Left Front

With smaller needles and A, cast on 28 (30, 34, 36, 40) sts.

Row 1 (RS): *K1, p1 rep from * across.

Rows 2 and 3: Rep Row 1.

Row 4: Work in pat to last st, inc 0 (1, 0, 1, 0). (28, 31, 34, 37, 40 sts)

Change to larger straight needles.

Row 5: Knit.

Row 6: Purl.

Rep Rows 5 and 6 until piece measures 10 inches, ending by working a WS.

Shape neck

Row 1: Knit to last 3 sts, k2 tog, k1. (27, 30, 33, 36, 39 sts)

Row 2: Purl.

Hilera 5: Derecho.

Hilera 6: Revés.

Rep Hileras 5 y 6 hasta que la pieza mida 20 (20½, 21, 21½, 22) pulgadas.

Cerrar 19 (21, 23, 25, 27) pts al inic de sig 2 hileras. (18, 20, 22, 24, 26 pts)

Cerrar pts restantes.

Frente Derecho

Con las agujas rectas más chicas y A, montar 28 (30, 34, 36, 40) pts.

Hilera 1 (LD): *Der1, rev1; rep desde * a lo largo.

Hileras 2 y 3: Rep Hilera 1.

Hilera 4: Aum 0 (1, 0, 1, 0) pts, trabajar puntada a lo largo. (28, 31, 34, 37, 40 pts)

Cambiar a agujas rectas grandes.

Hilera 5: Derecho.

Hilera 6: Revés.

Rep Hileras 5 y 6 hasta que la pieza mida 10 pulgadas, terminando con una hilera LR.

Formar cuello

Hilera 1 (LD): Der1, pst-pst-der, der hasta el final. (27, 30, 33, 36, 39 pts)

Hilera 2: Revés.

Continuar en p.jer, dism 1 pt en la orilla del cuello [cada 6a.hilera] 8 (9, 10, 11, 12) veces. (19, 21, 23, 25, 27 pts)

Trabajar uniformemente hasta que la pieza mida 20 (20½, 21, 21½, 22) pulgadas.

Cerrar.

Delantero Izq

Con las agujas más chicas y A, montar 28 (30, 34, 36, 40) pts.

Hilera 1 (LD): *Der1, rev1; rep desde * a lo largo.

Hileras 2 y 3: Rep Hilera 1.

Hilera 4: Trabajar puntada hasta ult pt, aum 0 (1, 0, 1, 0). (28, 31, 34, 37, 40 pts)

Cambiar a agujas rectas grandes.

Hilera 5: Derecho.

Hilera 6: Revés.

Rep Hileras 5 y 6 hasta que la pieza mida 10 pulgadas, terminando con una hilera LR.

Formar cuello

Hilera 1: Derecho hasta últimos 3 pts, der2jun, der1. (27, 30, 33, 36, 39 pts)

Hilera 2: Revés.

Continue in St st, dec 1 st at neck edge [every 6th row] 8 (9, 10, 11, 12) times. (19, 21, 23, 25, 27 sts)

Work even until piece measures 20 (20½, 21, 21½, 22) inches.

Bind off.

Sleeves

With smaller straight needles and A, cast on 30 (32, 34, 36, 38) sts.

Row 1 (RS): *K1, p1 rep from * across.

Rows 2–4: Rep Row 1.

Change to larger straight needles.

Work in St st (knit 1 row, purl 1 row) inc 1 st each edge [every 6th row] 10 (11, 11, 12, 12) times. (50, 54, 56, 60, 62 sts)

Work even in St st until sleeve measures 17 (17, 17½, 17½, 18) inches.

Bind off all sts.

Finishing

Sew shoulder seams. Place markers 8 (8½, 9, 9½, 10) inches on each side of shoulder seam. Matching center of sleeve to shoulder seam and edges to markers, sew in sleeve. Sew sleeve and side in continuous seam.

Front edgings

Note: *If not familiar with single crochet (sc) st, refer to crochet Stitch Guide on page 38.*

Right front edging

Hold with RS of right front facing, with crochet hook attach A at lower edge, work sc evenly spaced along front edge, from bottom of sweater to beg of V-neck shaping. Fasten off.

Left front Edging

Hold with RS of left front facing, with crochet hook attach A at beg of V-neck shaping, work sc evenly spaced along front edge, from V-neck of sweater to lower edge. Fasten off.

Collar

Row 1: Hold with WS facing, with smaller circular needle and B, pick up and knit 37 (39, 41, 43, 45) sts from beg of V-neck shaping to shoulder seam, pick up and knit 18 (20, 22, 24, 26) sts across back neck, pick up and knit 37 (39, 41, 43, 45) sts from shoulder seam to V-neck shaping. (92, 98, 104, 110, 116 sts)

Row 2: Knit.

Row 3: Knit.

Change to larger circular needles.

Continuar en p.jer, dism 1 pt en la orilla del cuello [cada 6a.hilera] 8 (9, 10, 11, 12) veces. (19, 21, 23, 25, 27 pts)

Trabajar uniformemente hasta que la pieza mida 20 (20½, 21, 21½, 22) pulgadas.

Cerrar.

Mangas

Con las agujas rectas más chicas y A, montar 30 (32, 34, 36, 38) pts.

Hilera 1 (LD): *Der1, rev1; rep desde * a lo largo.

Hileras 2-4: Rep Hilera 1.

Cambiar a agujas rectas grandes.

Trabajar en p.jer (der 1 hilera, rev 1 hilera) aum 1 pt cada orilla [cada 6a.hilera] 10 (11, 11, 12, 12) veces. (50, 54, 56, 60, 62 pts)

Trabajar uniformemente en p.jer hasta que la manga mida 17 (17, 17½, 17½, 18) pulgadas.

Cerrar todos los pts.

Acabado

Coser las costuras del hombro. Colocar marcadores 8 (8½, 9, 9½, 10) pulgadas en cada lado de la costura del hombro. Coser mangas, igualando el centro de la manga a la costura del hombro y las orillas a los marcadores. Coser manga y costado con una costura continua.

Orillas delanteras

Nota: *Referirse a la Guía de Puntos de crochet en la página 39.*

Orilla del frente derecho

Viendo LD de delantero der, con gancho de tejer unir A en orilla inferior, trabajar cs espaciados uniformemente a lo largo de orilla delantera, desde parte inferior del suéter hasta inic de forma cuello-V. Rematar.

Orilla del frente izquierdo

Viendo LD de delantero izq, con gancho de tejer unir A en inic. forma cuello-V, trabajar cs espaciados uniformemente a lo largo de orilla delantera, desde forma cuello-V del suéter hasta orilla inferior. Rematar.

Escote

Hilera 1: Viendo LR, con aguja circular pequeña y B, recoger y der 37 (39, 41, 43, 45) pts desde inic. cuello-V hasta la costura del hombro, recoger y der 18 (20, 22, 24, 26) pts a lo largo del cuello trasero, recoger y der 37 (39, 41, 43, 45) pts desde la costura del hombro hasta cuello-V. (92, 98, 104, 110, 116 pts)

Hilera 2: Derecho.

Hilera 3: Derecho.

Cambiar a agujas grandes circulares.

Rows 4–14: Sl 1k, k1, psso, k1, pass st on RH needle over k1, knit to last st, sl 1k.

Row 15: Knit.

Bind off all sts.

I-Cord Ties

Make 2

With A and dpn, cast on 3 sts. *K3, slide sts to right end of needle. Pull yarn across back of work. Rep from * until I-cord measures 8 inches.

Slide sts to end of needle and bind off.

Attach tassel to 1 end of I-cord. Sew opposite end of I-cord to front at beg of V-neck.

Hileras 4-14: Pst-d-p, der1, pasar pt sobre aguja MD sobre der1, der hasta último(s) pt, pst.

Hilera 15: Derecho.

Cerrar todos los pts.

Cordones

Hacer 2

Con A y aguja doble punto montar 3 pts. *Der3, pasar pts a orilla der de la aguja. Jalar estambre a lo largo de la parte de atrás del tejido. Rep desde * hasta que cordón mida 8 pulgadas.

Pasar pts a orilla de la aguja y cerrar.

Unir borla a 1 orilla del cordón. Coser orilla opuesta del cordón al frente al inic de cuello-V.

Light as Air Cropped Jacket

Saco Corto Ligero Como el Viento

Skill Level

EASY

Sizes

Woman's small (medium, large, extra-large, 2X-large) Instructions are given for smallest size with larger sizes in parentheses. When only 1 number is given, it applies to all sizes.

Finished Measurements

Chest: 36 (40, 44, 48, 52) inches

Materials

- Moda Dea Wild! bulky weight yarn (1.76 oz/103 yds/50g per skein): 3 (4, 4, 5, 6) skeins spring #9977 (A)
- Moda Dea Dream medium weight yarn (1.76 oz/93 yds/50g per skein): 1 skein leaf #3660 (B)
- Size 11 (8mm) knitting needles or size needed to obtain gauge
- Stitch holders
- Size J/10/6mm crochet hook
- Tapestry needle
- 2 natural shell pendants (optional)

5 BULKY

4 MEDIUM

Gauge

12 sts and 16 rows = 4 inches/10 cm in St st
To save time, take time to check gauge.

Nivel de dificultad

FÁCIL

Tallas

Dama chica (mediana, grande, extra-grande, 2X-grande) las instrucciones se muestran para talla chica, las demás tallas en paréntesis. Cuando sólo se indique un número, aplica para todas las tallas.

Medidas finales

Pecho: 36 (40, 44, 48, 52) pulgadas

Materiales

- Estambre Moda Dea Wild voluminoso (grueso) (1.76 oz., 103 yds, 50g por madeja); 3 (4, 4, 5, 6) madejas #9977 (A)
- Estambre Moda Dea Dream medio (estameña) (1.76 oz., 93 yds, 50g por madeja); 1 madeja #3660 (B)
- Agujas para tejer número 9 (5.5mm)
- Agujas para tejer número 11 (8mm) o medir para obtener la muestra del punto
- 2 sujeta puntos
- Gancho de tejer número J/10/6mm
- Aguja de tapicería
- 2 colgantes concha natural (opcional)

5 ABULTADO

4 MEDIO

Muestra de punto

12 pts y 16 hileras = 4 pulgadas /10 cm. en p.jer
Comprobar la muestra del punto.

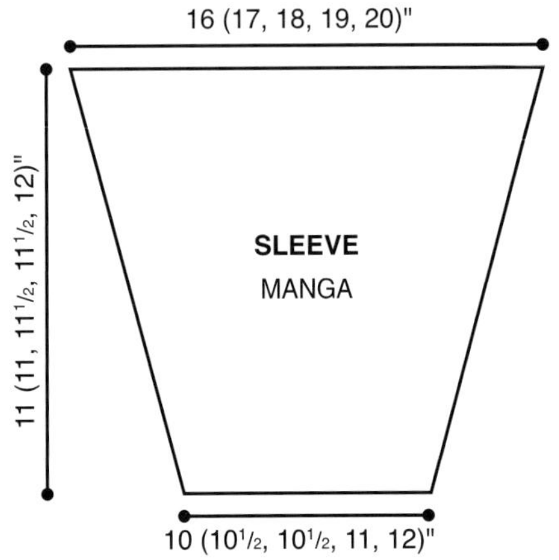

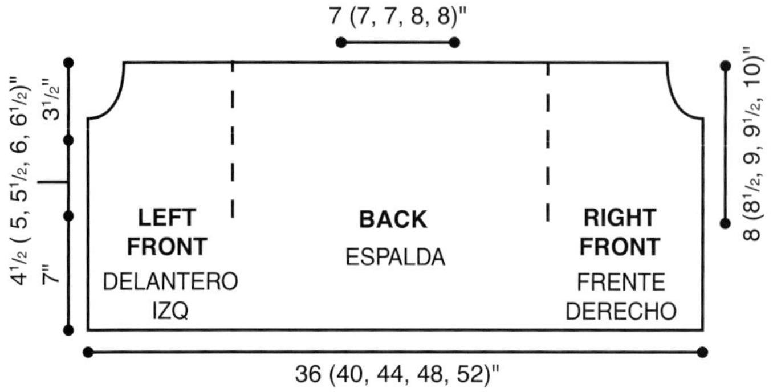

Body

Note: *Body is worked in one piece to underarms.*

With A, cast on 108 (120, 132, 144, 156) sts.

Row 1 (WS): Purl.

Row 2 (RS): Knit.

Rep Rows 1 and 2 until body measures 7 inches, ending with a WS row.

Right Front

Next row (RS): Knit 27 (30, 33, 36, 39) sts; sl next 54 (60, 66, 72, 78) sts onto holder for back; sl rem 27 (30, 33, 36, 39) sts onto st holder for left front.

Continue to work in St st until right front measures 11½ (12, 12½, 13, 13½) inches from beg, ending with a WS row.

Shape neck

Row 1 (RS): Bind off 7 (7, 7, 8, 8) sts knit across.

Row 2: Purl.

Row 3: K2 tog, knit across.

Rows 4–9: [Rep Rows 2 and 3] 3 times. (16, 19, 22, 24, 27 sts)

Row 10: Purl.

Work even in St st until armhole depth measures 8 (8½, 9, 9½, 10) inches.

Bind off.

Back

With A, knit 54 (60, 66, 72, 78) sts from st holder. Work even in St st until armhole measures same as Right Front.

Bind off.

Cuerpo

Nota: *El cuerpo se trabaja en una pieza hasta las sisas.*

Con A, montar 108 (120, 132, 144, 156) pts.

Hilera 1 (LR): Revés.

Hilera 2 (LD): Derecho.

Rep Hileras 1 & 2 hasta que el cuerpo mida 7 pulgadas, terminando con una hilera LR.

Frente Derecho

Siguiente hilera (LD): Der 27 (30, 33, 36, 39) pts, pst sig 54 (60, 66, 72, 78) pts al sujeta puntos para la espalda, pst rest 27 (30, 33, 36, 39) pts al sujeta puntos para delantero izq.

Continuar trabajando en p.jer hasta que delantero der mida 11½ (12, 12½,13, 13½) pulgadas desde inicio, terminando con una hilera LR.

Formar cuello

Hilera 1 (LD): Cerrar 7 (7, 7, 8, 8) pts der a lo largo.

Hilera 2: Revés.

Hilera 3: Der2jun, derecho a lo largo.

Hileras 4–9: [Rep Hileras 2 y 3] 3 veces. (16, 19, 22, 24, 27 pts)

Hilera 10: Revés.

Trabajar uniformemente en p.jer hasta que la profundidad de sisa mida 8 (8½, 9, 9½, 10) pulgadas.

Cerrar.

Espalda

Con A, derecho 54 (60, 66, 72, 78) pts del sujeta puntos. Trabajar uniformemente en p.jer hasta que la sisa mida lo mismo que el delantero der.

Cerrar.

Delantero Izq

Con A, derecho 27 (30, 33, 36, 39) pts del sujeta puntos.

Left Front

With A, knit 27 (30, 33, 36, 39) sts from st holder. Work even in St st until armhole measures same length as Right Front to neck shaping, ending with RS row.

Shape Neck

Row 1 (WS): Bind off 7 (7, 7, 8, 8) sts, purl across.

Row 2 (RS): Knit to last 2 sts, k2 tog.

Row 3: Purl.

Rows 4–9: [Rep Rows 2 and 3] 3 times. (16, 19, 22, 24, 27 sts)

Work even in St st until armhole measures 8 (8½, 9, 9½, 10) inches.

Bind off all sts.

Sleeves

With A, cast on 30 (32, 32, 34, 36) sts.

Row 1 (WS): Purl.

Row 2 (RS): Knit.

Rep Rows 1 and 2 inc 1 st each end [every 4th row] 9 (10, 11, 12, 12) times. (48, 52, 54, 58, 60 sts)

Work even until sleeve measures 11 (11, 11½, 11½, 12) inches.

Bind off.

Finishing

Sew shoulder seams leaving 7 (7, 7, 8, 8) inches at center back open. Sew sleeve seams. Matching center of sleeve to shoulder seam and sleeve seam to underarm, sew in sleeves.

Edgings

Note: *If not familiar with single crochet (sc) or chain (ch) refer to crochet Stitch Guide on page 38.*

Sleeve Edging

Beg at seam with crochet hook and B, work 2 rnds sc around lower sleeves. Fasten off.

Front Edging

Hold piece with lower edge at top, beg below either armhole with crochet hook and B, work 2 rnds sc around outer edge of jacket, working 3 sc in each corner. Fasten off.

Ties

Cut 2 (36-inch) lengths of B; thread 1 length through pendant. Fold yarn in half and with 2 strands held tog ch to end. Rep with other 36-inch length. Referring to photo, sew chains to each side of front neck.

Trabajar uniformemente en p.jer hasta la misma longitud que delantero der hasta base del cuello, terminando con hilera LD.

Formar cuello

Hilera 1 (LR): Cerrar 7 (7, 7, 8, 8) pts revés a lo largo.

Hilera 2 (LD): Derecho hasta últimos 2 pts, der2jun.

Hilera 3: Revés.

Hileras 4–9: [Rep Hileras 2 y 3] 3 veces. (16, 19, 22, 24, 27 pts)

Trabajar uniformemente en p.jer hasta que la sisa mida 8 (8½, 9, 9½, 10) pulgadas.

Cerrar todos los pts.

Mangas

Con A, montar 30 (32, 32, 34, 36) pts.

Trabajar 4 hileras en p.jer.

Continuar en p.jer aum 1 pt cada orilla [cada 4a hilera] 9 (10, 11, 12, 12) veces. (48, 52, 54, 58, 60 pts)

Trabajar uniformemente hasta que la manga mida 11 (11, 11½, 11½, 12) pulgadas.

Cerrar.

Acabado

Coser las costuras del hombro dejando 7 (7, 7, 8, 8) pulgadas abiertas al centro de la espalda. Coser las costuras de la manga. Coser mangas, igualando el centro de la manga a la costura del hombro y la costura de la manga a la sisa.

Orillas

Nota: *Referirse a la Guía de Puntos de crochet en la página 39.*

Orillas de la Manga

Inic en la costura, con gancho de tejer y B, trabajar 2 vtas cs alrededor del puño. Rematar.

Orillas del Frente

Sostener la pieza con la orilla inferior encima, inic abajo de cualquier sisa con gancho de tejer y B, trabajar 2 vtas cs alrededor de la orilla exterior del saco, trabajando 3 cs en cada esquina. Rematar.

Cierres

Cortar 2 hebras (36-pulgadas) de B. Cosa una hebra a través del colgante. Doble el estambre a la mitad y con 2 hilos una la cadena al final. Rep con la otra hebra de estambre. Como se ve en la fotografía, cosa las cadenas a cada lado del cuello por el frente.

Quick & Easy Tee

Skill Level

EASY

Sizes

Woman's small (medium, large, extra-large, 2X-large) Instructions are given for smallest size, with larger sizes in parentheses. When only 1 number is given, it applies to all sizes.

Finished Measurements

Chest: 36 (40, 44, 48, 52) inches

Materials

5 BULKY

- Moda Dea Ticker Tape bulky weight yarn (1.76 oz/67 yds/50g per ball): 8 (9, 10, 11, 12) balls tropical #9815
- Size 10 (6mm) straight and 16-inch circular knitting needles
- Size 11 (8mm) knitting needles or size needed to obtain gauge
- Stitch holders

Gauge

12 sts and 16 rows = 4 inches/10cm in St st with larger needles

To save time, take time to check gauge.

Back

Garter edge

With smaller straight needles, cast on 56 (62, 68, 74, 80) sts.

Work 8 rows in garter st.

Change to larger needles.

Body

Row 1 (RS): Knit.

Row 2: Purl.

Blusa Fácil y Rápida

Nivel de dificultad

FÁCIL

Tallas

Dama chica (mediana, grande, extra-grande, 2X-grande) Las Instrucciones se muestran para talla chica, las demás tallas en paréntesis. Cuando solo se indique un número, aplica para todas las tallas.

Medidas finales

Pecho: 36 (40, 44, 48, 52) pulgadas

Materiales

5 ABULTADO

- Estambre Moda Dea Ticker Tape voluminoso (1.76 oz/67 yds/50g por bola): 8 (9, 10, 11, 12) bolas tropical #9815
- Agujas para tejer rectas del número 10 (6mm) y circulares de 16-pulgadas
- Agujas para tejer número 11 (8mm) o medir para obtener la muestra del punto
- Sujeta puntos

Muestra de punto

12 pts y 16 hileras = 4 pulgadas/10cm en p.jer con agujas más grandes

Comprobar la muestra del punto.

Espalda

Orilla de punto musgo

Con las agujas rectas más chicas, montar 56 (62, 68, 74, 80) pts.

Trabajar 8 hileras en punto musgo.

Cambiar a agujas grandes.

Cuerpo

Hilera 1 (LD): Derecho.

Hilera 2: Revés.

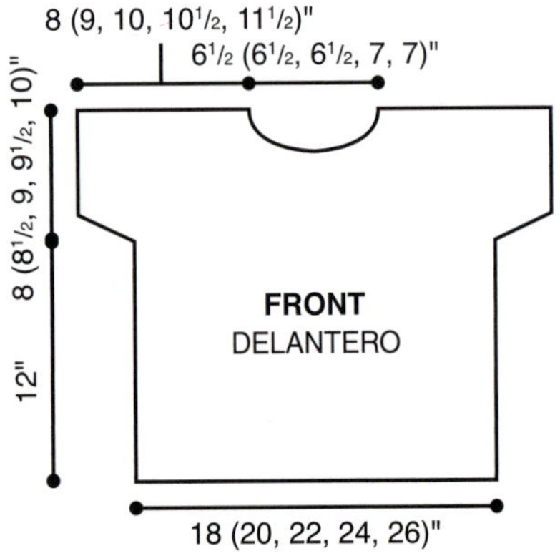

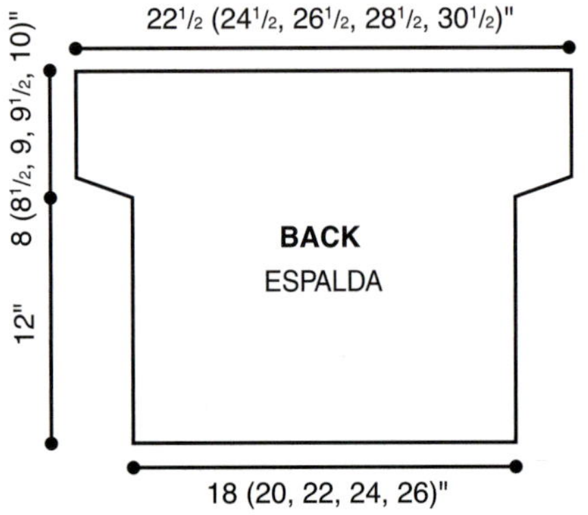

Rep Rows 1 and 2 until piece measures 12 inches, ending with a WS row.

Sleeves

Cast on 2 sts at beg of next 6 rows. (68, 74, 80, 86, 92 sts)

Work even until sleeve measures 8 (8½, 9, 9½, 10) inches, ending with a WS row.

Bind off 24 (27, 30, 32, 35) sts at beg of next 2 rows. Sl rem 20 sts (20, 20, 22, 22) sts onto holder.

Front

Work same as back until sleeve measures 4 (4½, 5, 5½, 6) inches, ending with a WS row.

Rep Hileras 1 y 2 hasta que la pieza mida 12 pulgadas, terminando con una hilera LR.

Mangas

Montar 2 pts al inic de sig 6 hileras. (68, 74, 80, 86, 92 pts)

Trabajar uniformemente hasta que la manga mida 8 (8½, 9, 9½, 10) pulgadas, terminando con hilera LR.

Cerrar 24 (27, 30, 32, 35) pts al inic de sig 2 hileras. Pst rest 20 pts (20, 20, 22, 22) pts al sujeta puntos.

Delantero

Trabajar igual que la espalda hasta que la manga mida 4 (4½, 5, 5½, 6) pulgadas, terminando con hilera LR.

Shape neck

Row 1: K25 (28, 31, 33, 36), k2tog, k1; place center 12 (12, 12, 14, 14) sts on st holder; attach 2nd ball of yarn; k1, ssk, k25 (28, 31, 33, 36) sts.

Row 2: Purl.

Row 3: K24 (27, 30, 32, 35), k2 tog, k1; k1, ssk, knit across.

Row 4: Purl.

Row 5: K23 (26, 29, 31, 34), k2 tog, k1; k1, ssk, knit across.

Row 6: Purl.

Row 7: K22 (25, 28, 30, 33), k2 tog, k1; k1, ssk, knit across. (24, 27, 30, 32, 35 sts on each side)

Row 8: Purl.

Work even until sleeve measures 8 (8½, 9, 9½, 10) inches, ending with WS row.

Bind off first side, knit across.

Bind off rem sts.

Assembly

Sew shoulder seams.

Edgings

Sleeve edging

Row 1: With smaller needles, pick up and knit 48 (52, 56, 60, 64) sts across lower edge of sleeve.

Rows 2–8: Knit.

Bind off.

Neck edging

Row 1: With smaller circular needle and beg at right shoulder seam, pick up and knit 20 (20, 20, 22, 22) sts from back neck holder, pick and knit 12 (14, 16, 18, 20) sts along left neck edge, pick up and knit 12 (12, 12, 14, 14) sts from front neck holder, pick up and knit 12 (14, 16, 18, 20) sts along right neck edge. (56, 60, 64, 72, 76 sts)

Row 2: Purl.

Row 3: Knit.

Rows 4 and 5: Rep Rows 2 and 3.

Row 6: Purl.

Bind off.

Finishing

Sew sleeve and side in one continuous seam.

Formar cuello

Hilera 1: Der25 (28, 31, 33, 36), der2jun, der1; colocar 12 (12, 12, 14, 14) pts centrales en sujeta puntos; unir 2a bola de estambre; der1, pst-pst-der, der25 (28, 31, 33, 36) pts.

Hilera 2: Revés.

Hilera 3: Der24 (27, 30, 32, 35), der2jun, der1; der1, pst-pst-der, derecho a lo largo.

Hilera 4: Revés.

Hilera 5: Der24 (26, 29, 31, 34), der2jun, der1; der1, pst-pst-der, derecho a lo largo.

Hilera 6: Revés.

Hilera 7: Der22 (25, 28, 30, 33), der2jun, der1; der1, pst-pst-der, derecho a lo largo. (24, 27, 30, 32, 35 pts en cada lado)

Hilera 8: Revés.

Trabajar uniformemente hasta que la manga mida 8 (8½, 9, 9½, 10) pulgadas, terminando con hilera LR.

Cerrar primer lado, derecho a lo largo.

Cerrar pts res.

Ensamblar

Coser las costuras del hombro.

Orillas

Orillas de la Manga

Hilera 1: Con ajugas más pequeñas, recoger y der 48 (52, 56, 60, 64) pts a lo largo de la orilla inferior de la manga.

Hileras 2-8: Derecho.

Cerrar.

Orilla del cuello

Hilera 1: Con aguja circular más pequeña e Inic en la costura del hombro derecho, recoger y der 20 (20, 20, 22, 22) pts del sujeta puntos de la parte trasera del cuello, recoger y der 12 (14, 16, 18, 20) pts a lo largo de la orilla izq del cuello, recoger y der 12 (12, 12, 14, 14) pts del sujeta puntos de la parte delantera del cuello, recoger y der 12 (14, 16, 18, 20) pts a lo largo de la orilla der del cuello. (56, 60, 64, 72, 76 pts)

Hilera 2: Revés.

Hilera 3: Derecho.

Hileras 4 y 5: Rep Hileras 2 y 3.

Hilera 6: Revés.

Cerrar.

Acabado

Coser manga y costado con una costura continua.

Must-Have Tunic

Túnica Tengo Que

Skill Level

EASY

Sizes

Woman's small (medium, large, extra-large, 2X-large) Instructions are given for smallest size, with larger sizes in parentheses. When only 1 number is given, it applies to all sizes.

Finished Measurements

Chest: 36 (40, 44, 48, 52) inches

Materials

- Patons Mosaic bulky weight yarn (1.75 oz/75 yds/50g per skein): 9 (10, 11, 12, 13) skeins pottery #12008
- Size 11 (8mm) knitting needles or size needed to obtain gauge
- Stitch holder

Gauge

14 sts and 18 rows = 4 inches/10cm in St st
To save time, take time to check gauge.

Back

Cast on 64 (70, 78, 84, 92) sts.

Row 1 (RS): Knit.

Row 2: Purl.

Rep Rows 1 and 2 until pieces measures 24 (24½, 25, 25½, 26) inches, ending with a WS row.

Bind off 21 (24, 27, 30, 33) sts at beg of next 2 rows. (22, 22, 24, 24, 26 sts)

Bind off.

Front

Cast on 64 (70, 78, 84, 92) sts.

Row 1 (RS): Knit.

Row 2: Purl.

Rep Rows 1 and 2 until piece measures 16 inches, ending with WS row.

Nivel de dificultad

FÁCIL

Tallas

Dama chica (mediana, grande, extra-grande, 2X-grande) Las Instrucciones se muestran para talla chica, las demás tallas en paréntesis. Cuando solo se indique un número, aplica para todas las tallas.

Medidas finales

Pecho: 36 (40, 44, 48, 52) pulgadas

Materiales

- Estambre Patons Mosaic voluminoso (1.75 oz/75 yds/50g por madeja): 9 (10, 11, 12, 13) madejas pottery #12008
- Agujas para tejer número 11 (8mm) o medir para obtener la muestra del punto
- Sujeta puntos

Muestra de punto

14 pts y 18 hileras = 4 pulgadas /10cm en p.jer
Comprobar la muestra del punto.

Espalda

Montar 64 (70, 78, 84, 92) pts.

Hilera 1 (LD): Derecho.

Hilera 2: Revés.

Rep Hileras 1 y 2 hasta que la pieza mida 24 (24½, 25, 25½, 26) pulgadas, terminando con una hilera LR.

Cerrar 21 (24, 27, 30, 33) pts al inic de sig 2 hileras. (22, 22, 24, 24, 26 pts)

Cerrar.

Delantero

Montar 64 (70, 78, 84, 92) pts.

Hilera 1 (LD): Derecho.

Hilera 2: Revés.

Rep Hileras 1 y 2 hasta que la pieza mida 16 pulgadas, terminando con una hilera LR.

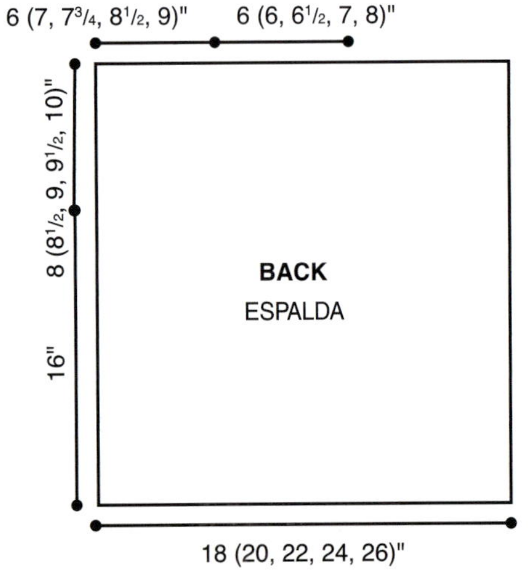

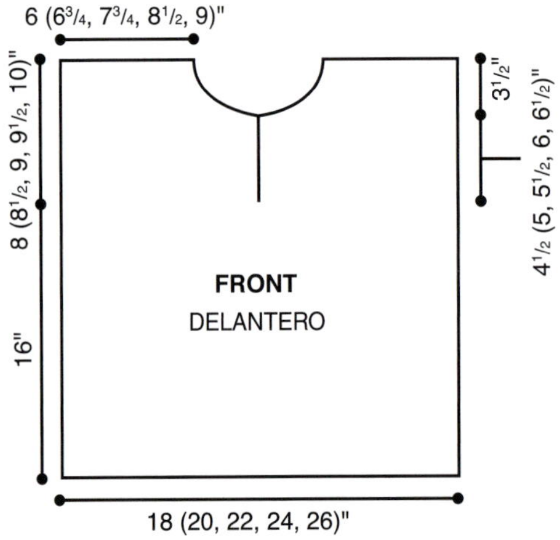

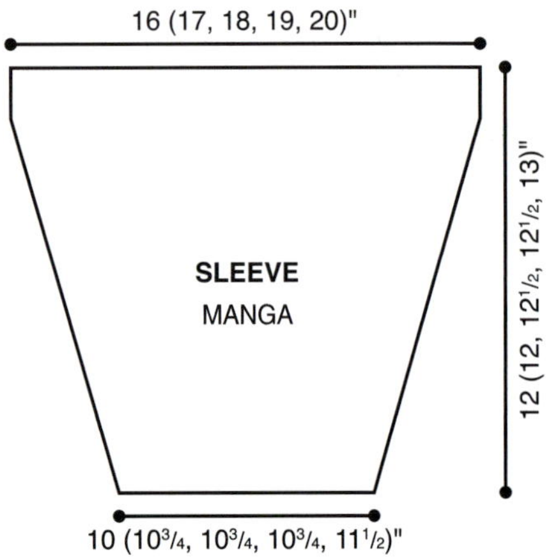

Shape left neck

Row 1 (RS): Knit 32 (35, 39, 42, 46) sts; place next 32 (35, 39, 42, 46) sts on holder.

Continue in St st, until neck opening measures 4½ (5, 5½, 6, 6½) inches, ending with a RS row.

Shape neckline

Row 1: Bind off 8 (8, 9, 9, 10) sts, purl across. (24, 27, 30, 33, 36 sts)

Row 2: Knit.

Row 3: P1, P2 tog, purl across.

[Rep Rows 2 and 3] twice. (21, 24, 27, 30, 33 sts)

Continue even in St st until neck opening measures 8 (8½, 9, 9½, 10) inches.

Bind off.

Shape right neck

Row 1: Knit 32 (35, 39, 42, 46) sts from st holder.

Work in St st, until neck opening measures 4½ (5, 5½, 6, 6½) inches, ending with a WS row.

Shape neckline

Row 1: Bind off 8 (8, 9, 9, 10) sts, knit across.

Row 2: Purl.

Row 3: K1, ssk, knit across.

[Rep Rows 2 and 3] twice. (21, 24, 27, 30, 33 sts)

Continue even in St st until neck opening measures 8 (8½, 9, 9½, 10) inches.

Bind off.

Sleeves

Cast on 36 (38, 38, 38, 40) sts.

Row 1: Knit.

Row 2: Purl.

Rows 3 and 4: Rep Rows 1 and 2.

Row 5: Inc, knit to last st, inc.

Sizes small & medium only

Continue in St st inc 1 st each edge [every 4th row] 9 (10) times. (56, 60 sts)

Continue with For All Sizes.

Sizes large, extra-large & 2X-large only

Continue in St st inc 1 st each edge [every 4th row] 6 (6, 7) times, then [every other row] 6 (7, 7) times. (64, 66, 70 sts)

Continue with For All Sizes.

Formar cuello izquierdo

Hilera 1 (LD): Der 32 (35, 39, 42, 46) pts; colocar sig 32 (35, 39, 42, 46) pts en sujeta puntos.

Continuar en p.jer hasta que apertura cuello mida 4½ (5, 5½, 6, 6½) pulgadas, terminando con una hilera LD.

Formar línea de cuello

Hilera 1: Cerrar 8 (8, 9, 9, 10) pts revés a lo largo. (24, 27, 30, 33, 36 pts)

Hilera 2: Derecho.

Hilera 3: Rev1, Rev2jun, rev a lo largo.

[Rep Hileras 2 y 3] 2 veces. (21, 24, 27, 30, 33 pts)

Continuar uniformemente en p.jer hasta que la apertura cuello mida 8 (8½, 9, 9½, 10) pulgadas.

Cerrar.

Formar cuello derecho

Hilera 1: Der 32 (35, 39, 42, 46) pts del sujeta puntos

Trabajar en p.jer hasta que apertura cuello mida 4½ (5, 5½, 6, 6½) pulgadas, terminando con una hilera LR.

Formar línea de cuello

Hilera 1: Cerrar 8 (8, 9, 9, 10) pts der a lo largo.

Hilera 2: Revés.

Hilera 3: Der1, pst-pst-der, der a lo largo.

[Rep Hileras 2 y 3] 2 veces. (21, 24, 27, 30, 33 pts)

Continuar uniformemente en p.jer hasta que la apertura cuello mida 8 (8½, 9, 9½, 10) pulgadas.

Cerrar.

Mangas

Montar 36 (38, 38, 38, 40) pts.

Hilera 1: Derecho.

Hilera 2: Revés.

Hileras 3 y 4: Rep Hileras 1 y 2.

Hilera 5: Aum, der hasta último pt, aum.

Tallas chica y mediana únicamente

Continuar en p.jer aum 1 pt cada orilla [cada 4a hilera] 9 (10) veces. (56, 60 pts)

Continuar con Para Todas las Tallas.

Tallas grande, extra-grande y 2X-grande únicamente

Continuar en p.jer aum 1 pt cada orilla [cada 4a hilera] 6 (6, 7) veces, después [cada tercer hilera] 6 (7, 7) veces. (64, 66, 70 pts)

Continuar con Para Todas las Tallas.

For All Sizes

Work even until sleeve measures 12 (12, 12½, 12½, 13) inches.

Bind off.

Finishing

Sew shoulder seams. Matching center of sleeve to shoulder seam, sew in sleeve. Sew sleeve and side in one continuous seam.

Para Todas las Tallas

Trabajar uniformemente hasta que la manga mida 12 (12, 12½, 12½, 13) pulgadas.

Cerrar.

Acabado

Coser las costuras del hombro. Igualar centro de la manga con costura del hombro, coser la manga. Coser manga y costado con una costura continua.

Easy-to-Wear V-Neck

Cuello en V Fácil de Usar

Skill Level

EASY

Sizes

Woman's small (medium, large, extra-large, 2X-large) Instructions are given for smallest size, with larger sizes in parentheses. When only 1 number is given, it applies to all sizes.

Finished Measurements

Chest: 38 (42, 46, 50, 54) inches

Materials

5 BULKY

- Moda Dea Vixen bulky weight yarn (1.76 oz/89 yds/50g per ball): 6 (7, 8, 9, 10) balls blue me away #3874
- Size 11 (8mm) knitting needles or size needed to obtain gauge
- Size G/6/4mm crochet hook
- Yarn needle

Nivel de dificultad

FÁCIL

Tallas

Dama chica (mediana, grande, extra-grande, 2X-grande) Las instrucciones se muestran para talla chica, las demás tallas en paréntesis. Cuando sólo se indique un número, aplica para todas las tallas.

Medidas finales

Pecho: 38 (42, 46, 50, 54) pulgadas

Materiales

5 ABULTADO

- Estambre Moda Dea Vixen voluminoso (1.76 oz/89 yds/50g por bola): 6 (7, 8, 9, 10) bolas blue me away #3874
- Agujas para tejer número 11 (8mm) o medir para obtener la muestra del punto
- Gancho de tejer número G/6/4mm
- Aguja gruesa para coser estambre

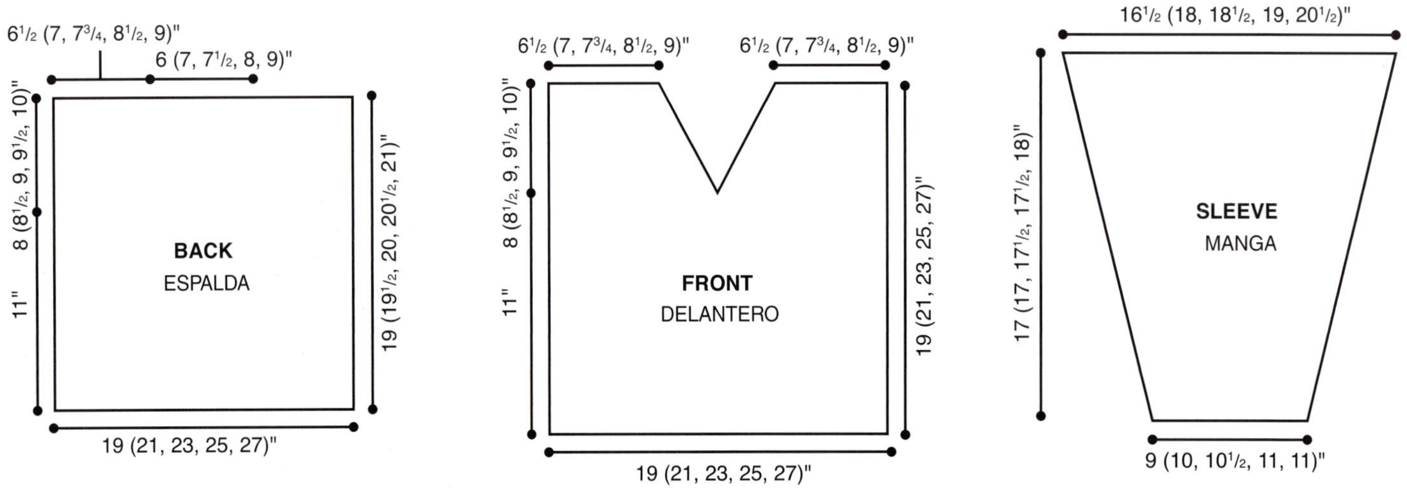

Gauge

12 sts and 18 rows = 4 inches/10 cm in St st

To save time, take time to check gauge.

Back

Cast on 57 (63, 69, 75, 81) sts.

Row 1 (WS): Purl.

Row 2 (RS): Knit.

Rep Rows 1 and 2 until piece measures 19 (19½, 20, 20½, 21) inches, ending with a WS row.

Bind off 19 (21, 23, 25, 27) sts at beg of 2 rows. (19, 21, 23, 25, 27 sts)

Bind off rem sts for back neck.

Front

Cast on 57 (63, 69, 75, 81) sts.

Row 1 (WS): Purl.

Row 2 (RS): Knit.

Rep Rows 1 and 2 until piece measures 11 inches, ending with a WS row.

Shape V-Neck

Row 1 (RS): K28 (31, 34, 37, 40); attach 2nd ball of yarn, bind off 1 st, knit rem sts.

Row 2: Working both sides at same time with separate balls of yarn, purl across.

Row 3: Knit to last 3 sts, k2 tog, k1; k1, ssk, knit across.

Row 4: Purl.

[Rep Rows 3 and 4] 8 (9, 10, 11, 12) times. (19, 21, 23, 25, 27 sts on each side)

Work even in St st until same length as back. Bind off rem sts on each side.

Sleeves

Cast on 28 (30, 32, 34, 34) sts.

Row 1 (WS): Purl.

Row 2 (RS): Knit.

Rep Rows 1 and 2, inc 1 st each edge [every 6th row] 11 (12, 12, 12, 14) times. (50, 54, 56, 58, 62 sts)

Work even in St st until sleeve measures 17 (17, 17½, 17½, 18) inches.

Bind off all sts.

Finishing

Sew shoulder seams. Place marker 8 (8½, 9, 9½, 10) inches from shoulder seam on front and back along armhole edge. Matching center of sleeve to shoulder seam and edges to markers, sew in sleeves. Sew side and sleeve in continuous seam.

Muestra de punto

12 pts y 18 hileras = 4 pulgadas/10 cm en p.jer

Comprobar la muestra del punto.

Espalda

Montar 57 (63, 69, 75, 81) pts.

Hilera 1 (LR): Revés.

Hilera 2 (LD): Derecho.

Rep Hileras 1 y 2 hasta que la pieza mida 19 (19½, 20, 20½, 21) pulgadas, terminando con una hilera LR.

Cerrar 19 (21, 23, 25, 27) pts al inic de 2 hileras. (19, 21, 23, 25, 27 pts)

Cerrar pts rest para cuello trasero.

Delantero

Montar 57 (63, 69, 75, 81) pts.

Hilera 1 (LR): Revés.

Hilera 2 (LD): Derecho.

Rep Hileras 1 y 2 hasta que la pieza mida 11 pulgadas, terminando con una hilera LR.

Formar Cuello-V

Hilera 1 (LD): Der28 (31, 34, 37, 40); unir 2a.bola de estambre, cerrar 1 pt, der pts rest.

Hilera 2: Trabajar ambos lados al mismo tiempo con bolas de estambre separadas, rev a lo largo.

Hilera 3: Derecho hasta últimos 3 pts, der2jun, der1; der1, pst-pst-der, der a lo largo.

Hilera 4: Revés.

[Rep Hileras 3 y 4] 8 (9, 10, 11, 12) veces. (19, 21, 23, 25, 27 pts en cada lado)

Trabajar uniformemente en p.jer hasta mismo largo que espalda. Cerrar pts rest. en cada lado.

Mangas

Montar 28 (30, 32, 34, 34) pts.

Hilera 1 (LR): Revés.

Hilera 2 (LD): Derecho.

Rep Hileras 1 y 2 aum 1 pt cada orilla [cada 6a hilera] 11 (12, 12, 12, 14) veces. (50, 54, 56, 58, 62 pts)

Trabajar uniformemente en p.jer hasta que la manga mida 17 (17, 17½, 17½, 18) pulgadas.

Cerrar todos los pts.

Acabado

Coser las costuras del hombro. Colocar marcador a 8 (8½, 9, 9½, 10) pulgadas desde la costura del hombro a lo largo de la orilla de la sisa delantera y trasera. Coser mangas, igualando el centro de la manga a la costura del hombro y las orillas a los marcadores. Coser costado y manga con una costura continua.

Edgings

***Note:** If not familiar with single crochet (sc) and chain (ch) sts, refer to crochet Stitch Guide on page 38.*

Lower edging

Rnd 1: Hold with RS facing, with crochet hook, attach yarn at 1 side seam, sc evenly around lower edge, having an even number of sts; join.

Rnd 2: *Ch 5, sk next sc, sl st in next ch; rep from * ending last sl st in beg sl st.

Fasten off.

Sleeve edging

Rnd 1: Hold with RS of 1 sleeve facing, with crochet hook, attach yarn at seam, sc evenly around edge of sleeve, having an even number of sts; join.

Rnd 2: *Ch 5, sk next sc, sl st in next sc; rep from * ending last sl st in beg sl st.

Fasten off.

Neck edging

Rnd 1: Hold with RS facing, with crochet hook, join yarn at 1 shoulder seam, sc evenly around neck edge, having an even number of sts; join

Rnd 2: *Ch 5, sk next sc, sl st in next sc; rep from * ending last sl st in beg sl st.

Fasten off and weave in all ends.

Orillas

***Nota:** Referirse a la Guía de Puntos de crochet en la página 39.*

Orilla inferior

Vta. 1: Viendo LD, con gancho de tejer, unir estambre a 1 costura lateral, cs uniformemente alrededor de orilla inferior, quedando número par de pts; unir.

Vta. 2: *Cad 5, saltar sig cs, p.desl sig cad; rep desde * terminando ult p.desl en p.desl inic.

Rematar.

Orillas de la Manga

Vta. 1: Viendo LD de 1 manga, con gancho de tejer, unir estambre a costura, cs uniformemente alrededor de orilla de manga, quedando número par de pts; unir.

Vta. 2: *Cad 5, saltar sig cs, p.desl sig cs; rep desde * terminando ult p.desl en p.desl inic.

Rematar.

Orilla del cuello

Vta. 1: Viendo LD, con gancho de tejer, unir estambre a 1 costura hombro, cs uniformemente alrededor de orilla cuello, quedando número par de pts; unir.

Vta. 2: *Cad 5, saltar sig cs, p.desl sig cs; rep desde * terminando ult p.desl en p.desl inic.

Rematar y entretejer todos los extremos sueltos.

How to Check Gauge

A correct stitch gauge is very important. Please take the time to work a stitch gauge swatch about 4 x 4 inches. Measure the swatch. If the number of stitches and rows are fewer than indicated under "Gauge" in the pattern, your needles are too large. Try another swatch with a smaller size hook. If the number of stitches and rows are more than indicated under "Gauge" in the pattern, your hook is too small. Try another swatch with larger size needles.

Muestra de punto

Antes de iniciar, es importante hacer un cuadro de muestra de punto de aproximadamente 4 pulgadas con el patrón y las agujas recomendadas.

Mida la muestra. Si el número de puntos y líneas son menos que las indicadas en "Muestra del punto" en el patrón, las agujas que se están utilizando son muy grandes. Haga otra muestra con agujas más chicas. Si el número de puntos y líneas son más que las indicadas en "Muestra del punto" en el patrón, las agujas que se están utilizando son muy pequeñas. Haga otra muestra con agujas más grandes.

Continúe ajustando el tamaño de las agujas hasta lograr la muestra de punto correcta.

Skill Levels

Niveles de Dificultad

BEGINNER
Beginner projects for first-timers using basic stitches. Minimal shaping.

EASY
Easy projects using basic stitches, repetitive stitch patterns, simple color changes and simple shaping and finishing.

INTERMEDIATE
Intermediate projects with a variety of stitches, mid-level shaping and finishing.

EXPERIENCED
Experienced projects using advanced techniques and stitches, detailed shaping and refined finishing.

PRINCIPIANTE
Proyectos para principiantes, utilizando puntadas Básicas. Mínima necesidad de dar forma al tejido.

FÁCIL
Proyectos sencillos utilizando puntadas Básicas, patrones de puntadas repetitivos, cambios de color simples y forma y acabados sencillos.

INTERMEDIO
Proyectos intermedios con una variedad de puntadas, forma y acabados de media dificultad.

AVANZADO
Proyectos más experimentados utilizando técnicas y puntadas avanzadas, forma detallada y acabados delicados.

Standard Yarn Weight System

Sistema de Peso Standard para Estambre

Categories of yarn, gauge ranges, and recommended needle sizes

Yarn Weight Symbol & Category Names	1 SUPER FINE	2 FINE	3 LIGHT	4 MEDIUM	5 BULKY	6 SUPER BULKY
	1 SÚPER FINO	2 FINO	3 LIGERO	4 MEDIO	5 ABULTADO	6 SÚPER ABULTADO
Type of Yarns in Category	Sock, Fingering, Baby	Sport, Baby	DK, Light Worsted	Worsted, Afghan, Aran	Chunky, Craft, Rug	Bulky, Roving
Knit Gauge Range* in Stockinette Stitch to 4 inches	27–32 sts	23–26 sts	21–24 sts	16–20 sts	12–15 sts	6–11 sts
Recommended Needle in Metric Size Range	2.25–3.25 mm	3.25–3.75 mm	3.75–4.5 mm	4.5–5.5 mm	5.5–8 mm	8 mm and larger
Recommended Needle U.S. Size Range	1 to 3	3 to 5	5 to 7	7 to 9	9 to 11	11 and larger

* GUIDELINES ONLY: The above reflect the most commonly used gauges and needle sizes for specific yarn categories.

Abbreviations & Symbols

approx .... approximately
beg .... begin(ning)
CC .... contrasting color
cn .... cable needle
dec .... decrease/decreases/decreasing
g .... gram
inc .... increase/increases/increasing
k .... knit
k2tog .... knit 2 stitches together
LH .... left hand
lp(s) .... loop(s)
M1 .... make one stitch
MC .... main color
mm .... millimeter(s)
oz .... ounce(s)
p .... purl
pat(s) .... pattern(s)
p2tog .... purl 2 stitches together
psso .... pass slipped stitch over
rem .... remain(ing)
rep .... repeat(s)
rev St st .... reverse stockinette stitch
RH .... right hand
rnd(s) .... round(s)
RS .... right side
sl .... slip
sl 1k .... slip 1 knitwise
sl 1p .... slip 1 purlwise
sl st .... slip stitch(es)
ssk .... slip, slip, knit these 2 stitches together–a decrease
ssp .... slip, slip, purl these 2 stitches together–a decrease
st(s) .... stitch(es)
St st .... stockinette stitch
tbl .... through back loop
tog .... together
WS .... wrong side
wyib .... with yarn in back
wyif .... with yarn in front
yd(s) .... yard(s)
yfwd .... yarn forward
yo .... yarn over

[ ] work instructions within brackets as many times as directed
( ) work instructions within parentheses in the place directed
* repeat instructions following the single asterisk as directed
" inch(es)

Abreviaturas

aa .... aguja auxiliary
adp .... aguja de doble punto
aum .... aumentar(a)(ando)
cad .... cadeneta
CC .... color contrastante
der .... derecho
der2jun .... tejer derecho 2 puntos juntos
dism .... disminuir(e)(yendo)
inic .... iniciar/inicio
izq .... izquierdo
jun .... juntos
LD .... lado derecho
LR .... lado revés
MD .... mano derecha
p.desl. .... p.deslizado
p.jer .... punto de jersey
ppe .... pasar por encima
pst .... pasar sin tejer
pst-d-p .... pasar 1 sin tejer, tejer 1 derecho, ... pasar el punto sin tejer por encima
pst-pst-der .... pasar sin tejer, pasar sin tejer, derecho
pst-r-p .... pasar 1 sin tejer, tejer 1 revés, ... pasar el punto sin tejer por encima
pt(s) .... punto(s)
rep .... repetir
res .... restante(s)
rest .... el resto
rev .... revés
rev2jun .... tejer revés 2 puntos juntos
sig .... siguiente(s)
ult .... últimos(a)(s)(as)
vta(s) .... vuelta(s)

Tejido de crochet
cs .... crochet sencillo

[ ] trabajar las instrucciones entre corchetes tantas veces como se indique
( ) trabajar las instrucciones entre paréntesis en el lugar indicado
* repetir las instrucciones después de un asterisco como se indique
" pulgada(s)

Stitch Guide

Chain—ch:
YO, draw through lp on hook.

Single Crochet—sc:
Insert hook in st, yo and draw through, yo and draw through both lps on hook.

Reverse Single Crochet—Reverse sc:
Work from left to right, insert hook in sp or st indicated (**a**), draw lp through sp or st - 2 lps on hook (**b**); yo and draw through lps on hook.

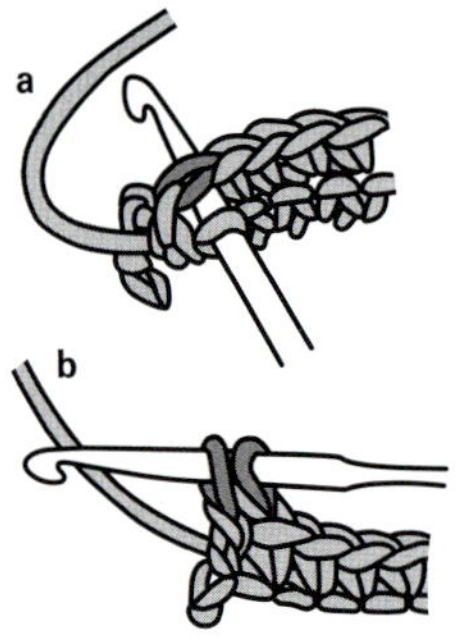

Half Double Crochet—hdc:
yo, insert hook in st, yo, draw through, yo and draw through all 3 lps on hook.

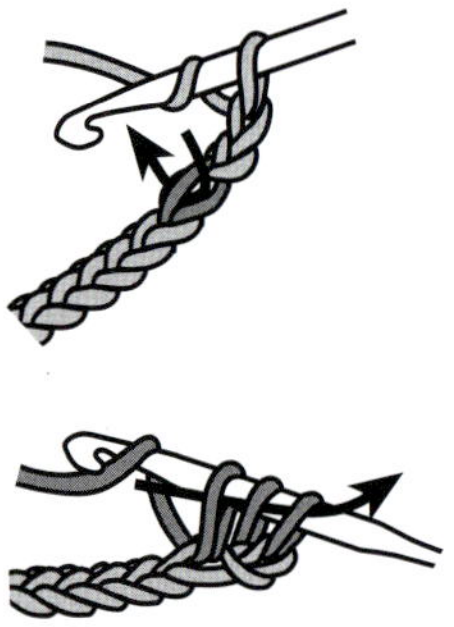

Double Crochet—dc:
yo, insert hook in st, yo, draw through, (yo and draw through 2 lps on hook) twice.

Triple Crochet—trc:
yo twice, insert hook in st, yo, draw through, (yo and draw through 2 lps on hook) 3 times.

Slip Stitch—sl st:
(**a**) **Used for Joinings**
Insert hook in indicated st, yo and draw through st and lp on hook.

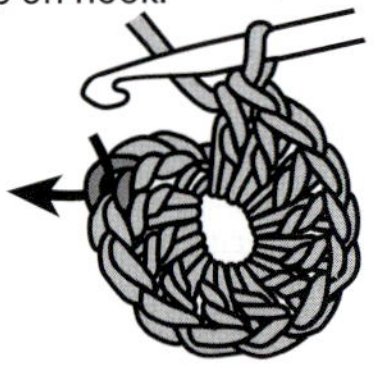

(**b**) **Used for Moving Yarn Over**
Insert hook in st, yo draw through st and lp on hook.

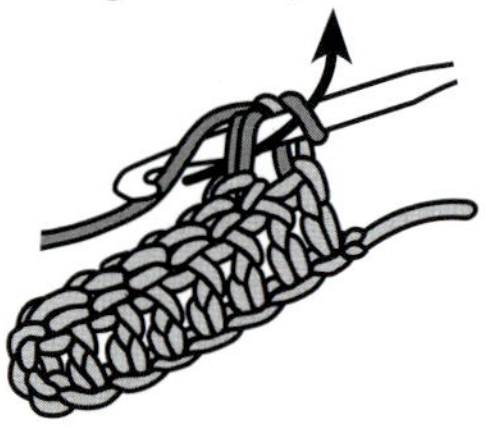

Front Loop—FL:
The front loop is the loop toward you at the top of the stitch.

Back Loop—BL:
The back loop is the loop away from you at the top of the stitch.

Post:
The post is the vertical part of the stitch.

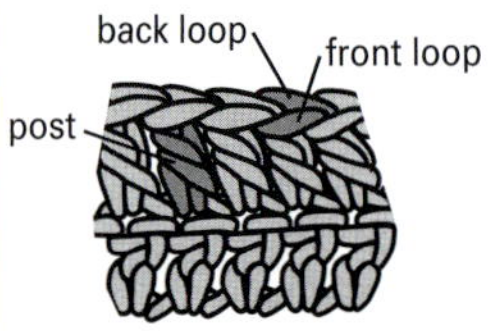

Overcast Stitch is worked loosely to join crochet pieces.

Puntadas

Cadena—Cad:
Ppe, sacar a través de lazada del gancho.

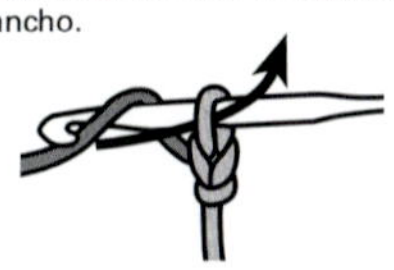

Crochet Sencillo (Medio Punto)—Cs:
Insertar gancho en el pt, ppe y sacar lazada, ppe y sacar las 2 lazadas del gancho.

Crochet Sencillo Revés (Punto Cangrejo)—Cs Revés:
Trabajar de izquierda a derecha, insertar gancho en esp o pt indicado (a), sacar lazada a través de esp o pt—2 lazadas en el gancho (b); ppe y sacar las lazadas 2 del gancho.

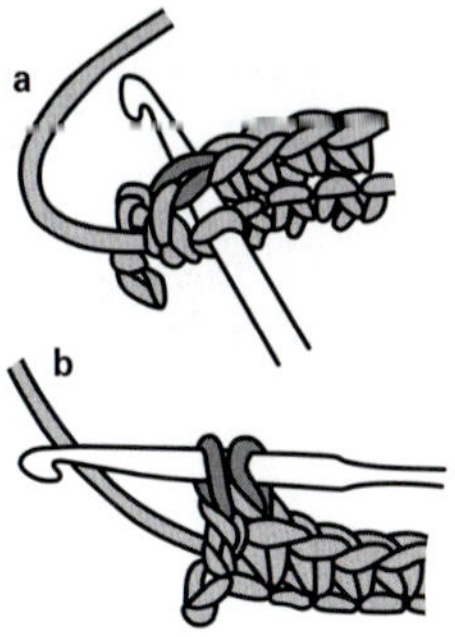

Medio Crochet Doble (medio punto entero)—Mcd:
Ppe, insertar gancho en el pt, ppe y sacar lazada, ppe y sacar las 3 lazadas del gancho.

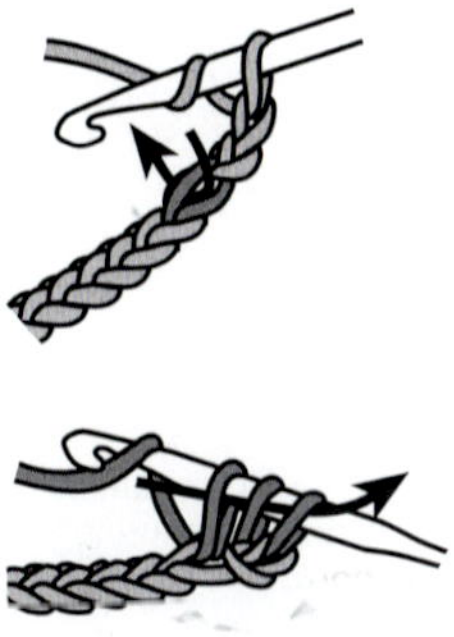

Crochet Doble (Punto Entero)—Cd:
Ppe, insertar gancho en el pt, ppe y sacar lazada, (ppe y sacar 2 lazadas del gancho) 2 veces.

Crochet Triple (Punto Alto Triple)—Ctr:
Ppe 2 veces, insertar gancho en el pt, ppe y sacar lazada, (ppe y sacar 2 lazadas del gancho) 3 veces.

Punto Deslizado—P.desl:
(a) Utilizado para Uniones
Insertar gancho en pt indicado, ppe y sacar el pt y la lazada del gancho.

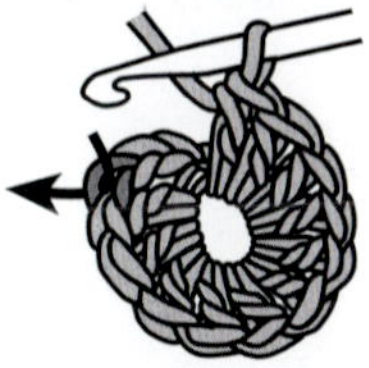

(b) Utilizado para Cambiar el Estambre de Posición
Insertar gancho en pt, ppe y sacar el pt y la lazada del gancho.

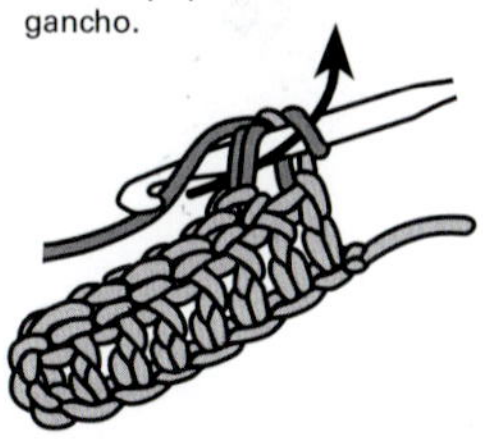

Lazada Delantera—SLD:
La lazada delantera es la lazada hacia usted en la parte superior del punto.

Lazada Trasera—SLT:
La lazada trasera es la lazada contra usted en la parte superior del punto.

Poste o Palo:
El palo es la parte vertical del punto.

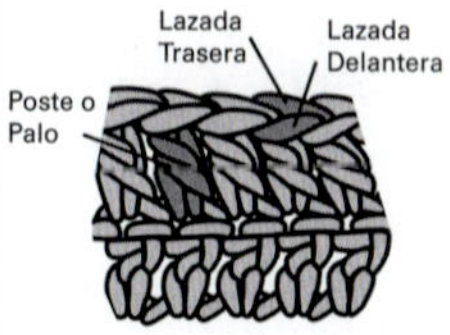

El Punto por Encima se trabaja suelto para unir pts de tejido.

Metric Chart

Sistema Métrico

INCHES INTO MILLIMETERS & CENTIMETERS (Rounded off slightly)

inches	mm	cm	inches	cm	inches	cm	inches	cm
1/8	3	0.3	5	12.5	21	53.5	38	96.5
1/4	6	0.6	5 1/2	14	22	56	39	99
3/8	10	1	6	15	23	58.5	40	101.5
1/2	13	1.3	7	18	24	61	41	104
5/8	15	1.5	8	20.5	25	63.5	42	106.5
3/4	20	2	9	23	26	66	43	109
7/8	22	2.2	10	25.5	27	68.5	44	112
1	25	2.5	11	28	28	71	45	114.5
1 1/4	32	3.2	12	30.5	29	73.5	46	117
1 1/2	38	3.8	13	33	30	76	47	119.5
1 3/4	45	4.5	14	35.5	31	79	48	122
2	50	5	15	38	32	81.5	49	124.5
2 1/2	65	6.5	16	40.5	33	84	50	127
3	75	7.5	17	43	34	86.5		
3 1/2	90	9	18	46	35	89		
4	100	10	19	48.5	36	91.5		
4 1/2	115	11.5	20	51	37	94		

KNITTING NEEDLES CONVERSION CHART

U.S.	0	1	2	3	4	5	6	7	8	9	10	10 1/2	11	13	15
Metric(mm)	2	2 1/4	2 3/4	3 1/4	3 1/2	3 3/4	4	4 1/2	5	5 1/2	6	6 1/2	8	9	10

American School of Needlework® excellence in instruction

DRG Publishing
306 East Parr Road
Berne, IN 46711

TOLL-FREE ORDER LINE
or to request a free catalog (800) 582-6643
Customer Service (800) 282-6643, **Fax** (800) 882-6643
Visit AnniesAttic.com.

LINEA SIN CARGO PARA PEDIDOS o para ordenar un catálogo gratuito (800) 582-6643
Servicio a Clientes (800) 282-6643, **Fax** (800) 882-6643
Visite www.AnniesAttic.com.

1 2 3 4 5 6 7 8 9

ISBN 10: 1-59012-162-7
ISBN 13: 978-1-59012-162-7